Altared

Altared

A Tale of
Renovating a
Medieval Church
in Tuscany

KYLE TACKWELL BALL

SHE WRITES PRESS

Originally published as an ebook in 2020
Published 2022
Printed in the United States of America
Paperback ISBN: 978-1-64742-078-9
Hardcover ISBN: 978-1-64742-078-9
E-ISBN: 978-1-64742-053-6
Library of Congress Control Number: 2022904951

For information, address:
She Writes Press
1569 Solano Ave #546
Berkeley, CA 94707

Interior design by Tabitha Lahr

She Writes Press is a division of SparkPoint Studio, LLC.

With gratitude and much love to:

My husband, Chuck, who supported me throughout the years' long purchase process and renovation of Le Convertoie. "If I were you, I would have divorced me by now . . ."

To our dear friends Sue Scranton Capitani and Fabio Capitani. This would never have been possible without you. *Grazie mille!*

To our children, Josh and Tracy, and daughter-in-law, Liz. Thanks for never reminding me how much this was cutting into your inheritance.

CONTENTS

i am a little church (no great cathedral)
far from the splendor and squalor
of hurrying cities—i do not worry if briefer days grow briefest,
i am not sorry when sun and rain make april

my life is the life of the reaper and the sower;
my prayers are prayers of earth's own clumsily striving
(finding and losing and laughing and crying)
children whose any sadness or joy is my grief or my gladness

around me surges a miracle of unceasing
birth and glory and death and resurrection:
over my sleeping self float flaming symbols
of hope, and i wake to a perfect patience of mountains

i am a little church (far from the frantic
world with its rapture and anguish) at peace with nature
—i do not worry if longer nights grow longest;
i am not sorry when silence becomes singing

winter by spring, I lift my diminutive spire to
merciful Him Whose only now is forever:
standing erect in the deathless truth of His presence
(welcoming humbly His light and proudly His darkness)

—e. e. cummings[1]

PROLOGUE

A hard rain drove through the open rafters, trickling down the ancient, plastered walls and gathering in puddles around the bare cement altar. It had been pouring for days in Tuscany, with harsh winds bending the brittle limbs of the olive trees and endless rivers of water rushing down the vineyard rows. I stood in the center of the roofless ruin with an umbrella, soaked to the bone, praying for a break in the weather. "What was I thinking?" had become my constant refrain since renovation began on the ancient *chiesa*, or church. Destined to become a living room at some point in my natural lifetime, it was hard to imagine the space, fully open to the elements, becoming livable in the foreseeable future. Why I had been drawn to buy a church in Italy was still a mystery to me, and the place seemed to have taken on a life of its own. The endless red tape and setbacks felt like I had stepped into cultural quicksand, and I was in way over my head.

I had begun a search for property in Italy with a vision of a quaint country home near Florence—a charming stone farmhouse, move-in ready with arched windows, beamed ceilings, and terracotta-tiled floors. I ended up starring in a "Stones and Bones" classic, purchasing an abandoned chapel requiring years of renovation, monumental permitting issues, and mountains of cash, and featuring a resident ghost with a penchant for Marlboro Lights.

Is fate a factor when buying a property? The emotions that washed over me when I saw the ruined church for the first time were raw and fluid. Like a moth to a flame, the challenges the project presented had an extraordinary pull: magnetic, serendipitous, irrefutable, and irresistible. It was as if it had selected me—not the other way around. I knew I could resurrect it, although I didn't understand at that moment that the baptism would be by fire, not water. A restoration of this magnitude would take a lot of time, an unlimited budget, and a much better command of the Italian language than I possessed. In fact, I didn't speak much Italian at all. But my epiphany was complete the moment I set eyes on it, and the rest, as they say, is history.

THE EPIPHANY

I had been longing to own a home in Italy for years and sheepishly admit I was influenced by Frances Mayes's wildly popular story of her own experiences renovating a house in Italy, *Under the Tuscan Sun*.[2] My husband, Chuck, and I had lived overseas in the 1980s—four years in London and three years in Brussels—so we were familiar with the challenges of life in a foreign country. Two of my closest friends had studied abroad and married Italians. Sue, Lou (Marie Louise), and I stayed in touch after college, and my family had visited them frequently, often staying with Lou and her then-husband, Stefano, in his villa in the hills outside of Florence. The idyllic weekends we enjoyed there, with Sunday lunches savored at the quintessential long, wooden table accompanied by local Chianti poured from straw-covered bottles, rivaled scenes from *A Room with a View*.

Chuck was *un pò freddo* (unenthusiastic) about the adventure. He expressed a strong preference for a vacation home where he could understand the language, play golf, and retain some liver function during his golden years. None of those were likely if we bought a house in Italy. But in the fall of 2000, with our son and daughter in college and my empty nest syndrome in overdrive, I was given the green light for an exploratory real estate excursion to *la Bella Italia.* Since Chuck was busy working stateside—someone had to pay for this—I asked a friend to join me. Famous for her shopping and Italian 101 language skills from a study abroad program years ago, Betsy was an ideal choice for a traveling companion, and she and I headed to Florence on a scouting trip. One of my more prominent personality traits is that I don't scout for much at all—if I'm looking, I'm buying. A friend once described me in this way: "Kyle shops like a terrorist. She's in, she's out, and things get blown up sometimes, but she gets it done." This description aptly describes my approach to many facets of life, and no one really believed I was going on an "exploratory" house hunt.

My first initiation into the Italian real estate system was discovering that there isn't a system at all, something I would learn was true of life in Italy in general. There is no comprehensive multi-list you can search. *Stranieri* (foreigners) who are prospective buyers work with a number of different agents in order to see available properties. Italians rarely do that. They know someone who can make discreet inquiries about properties that are not yet listed but might be for sale.

Sue and her Florentine-native husband, Fabio, served as the advance team before Betsy and I arrived and recommended focusing the search around Greve, described as "the heart of Chianti." We had decided against living in the congested Florence city center, and a small town within easy driving distance seemed to be a good alternative. Greve is a charming village with an attractive central square called Piazza Matteotti. In addition to the outstanding wines it's justly famous for, it is the birthplace of the sixteenth-century explorer Giovanni da Verrazzano. In 1528, Verrazzano's illustrious career came to an abrupt halt when he was eaten by natives in the Caribbean. Maybe that should have served as a cautionary, although less tropical, tale for me? Bars of the Italian variety, where neighbors sip espresso, catch up on local gossip, or enjoy an afternoon *aperitivo* surround the piazza. History abounds in Greve, with the nearby Villa Vignamaggio reputed to be where Leonardo da Vinci painted the portrait of Lisa Gherardini, known as the *Mona Lisa*, in the early 1500s. I happily agreed to Sue and Fabio's suggestion to look in Greve, since it seemed to fit all our criteria. Only thirty minutes south of Florence on the SS 222 or Chiantigiana Road, Greve is perfectly situated for day trips to some of the area's most notable Tuscan hill towns: Siena, San Gimignano, Volterra, and Ms. Mayes's adopted city of Cortona. A steady influx of British expats nicknamed the area "Chiantishire," and many of the area's residents and shopkeepers speak English.

Sue and Fabio introduced me to a real estate agent in Greve named Marinella Coppi, who had several homes in the area she thought might be of interest. As we met in the piazza that morning, I felt an instant rapport with Marinella. Petite and attractive, with auburn hair and huge brown eyes, she exuded an air of trustworthiness and had a charming cadence to her English. As Marinella, Betsy, and I climbed into her car for the short drive up into the hills outside of Greve, Marinella explained the unusual situation surrounding the first property we were to see. It was an apartment, not a house, part of an attached building located in a historic *borgo* or village. "I am sure you will like it, but it is not really for sale," she assured me. "There is a small problem between the brothers who jointly own the property, but these issues can be easily resolved."

Everyone has defining moments in life. Time stands still; you realize that you should listen to the warning bell ringing loudly in your ears, but you jump in anyway. This internal warning signal should go off whenever any Italian uses the phrase "easily resolved," but I naively thought there was no harm in looking.

The drive from the piazza took us past the local *farmacia* (pharmacy) down a winding road through a lovely stretch of vineyards. We made a sharp left and headed down a narrow gravel path threading between tidy rows of olive trees, abruptly ending up in a parking area that could have served as the backdrop for a European version of *Hoarders*.

"*Eccola!*" announced Marinella.

The area was strewn with a haphazard array of farm equipment in varying states of decay. A rusty wheelbarrow, its front wheel missing, sat impotently next to a mailbox perched at a steep pitch on its post. An ancient Jeep, its roof and hood covered in mud and bird droppings, was parked under the shade of a cypress tree. Two large dogs, one a fierce looking terrier mix and the other a German shepherd, rushed the car barking ferociously in a bid to scare us off from what was clearly their domain. We had arrived at Le Convertoie!

Consisting of three individually owned villas, including a renovated stable, an abandoned church, and two apartments in the main building connected by a staircase and corridor, the *borgo* was typical of many in Tuscany. In medieval times, they had served as feudal farms owned by wealthy landowners. As was the case with Le Convertoie, many had been fortified to protect the residents who had lived and farmed there from the thirteenth century. The hamlet was then known as Ripamortoia, an estate on an ancient Etruscan route mentioned in historical annals as far back as 1260.

Backing slowly away from the car and the dogs, Marinella, Betsy, and I headed up the steep hill toward the entrance, where the aroma of freshly baked bread drew us through a tall wooden door. Veering down a dark corridor, we were greeted with the mingling aromas of fermenting yeast and espresso. As we entered, we encountered an elderly woman slowly turning the baking loaves, the rhythmic sound of her paddle scraping the bottom of the wood-burning oven in the wall of the tiny alcove. Her short, snow-white hair was tied in a printed kerchief, and she was dressed in black from head to toe, giving the distinct impression she'd just stepped out of another century. Sweat poured off her brow, and when she turned to greet us, she gave us a begrudging grin and a brief "*Buongiorno*."

"That's Bianca" explained Marinella. "She bakes bread here and sells it to a select group of local clients."

Bianca looked none too pleased at the interruption and turned back to the task at hand. We walked on through the corridor to a set of rustic wooden doors that led into the apartment. As we entered, sunlight poured through two sets of arched windows and a glass door leading out to the garden, warming the terracotta floors with a welcoming glow. The ceiling was typically Tuscan—rough-hewn timber beams interspersed with slabs of stucco—and there were two doors at the far end of the room, one leading to a small closet, the other opening curiously to a concrete wall. The garden was overgrown and neglected, but it had pretty views of the surrounding hills.

At one end of the kitchen stood a huge stone fireplace, its hearth blackened from years of use and a date of 1876 etched in the arched backsplash. An ancient stone trough sat underneath a small window, contrasting with the kitchen, which had a modern stainless steel sink decorated with curious "dancing teacup" tiles. A steep staircase led from the kitchen down to the cantina with ten-foot thick walls, where wine is stored, and which Marinella explained had been used as a safe haven for villagers during World War II bombings. A moldy leg of prosciutto hung from an iron hook in the center of the room. A flip of the switch for the single naked light bulb dangling from the ceiling revealed spiders scurrying between an intricate series of webs throughout the room. A tiny window at the far end of the cantina was so dirty that light filtered through it in sudden bursts of brown and gold.

Upstairs, there were three bedrooms and two baths, both in need of updating, but the floors were fashioned out of a gorgeous, highly polished olive wood. The layout was odd, with a door leading to a separate apartment—in old farmhouses, occupants would simply add rooms as needed. Three brick steps led up to a landing and then back down into the largest of the bedrooms. The shuttered windows had been opened to reveal a vine-covered villa next door that was so close you could almost reach out and touch it.

As we looked through the apartment, I asked Marinella why the owner was selling. It had clearly been vacant for some time, yet this was a busy, productive farm. She paused for a moment, struggling to gather her thoughts into English. "Two brothers once lived in the separate apartments with their families. After each divorced and remarried, some conflicts arose, and the younger brother moved out. His older brother still lives upstairs with his wife and son, and his mother, Bianca, helps them around the property, a very common arrangement in Italy." Mari continued, "There are some minor issues that need to be ironed out, since there was a shared corridor along with a common electrical, sewer, and water service." But, she reassured me, "These things can easily be resolved!"

Betsy and I were confused, as the apartment was much smaller than what I was looking for, plus it seemed as if any potential buyer would be asking for trouble. Asked why she had decided to show it to me, Marinella replied, "This property has an interesting building that I think you should see."

She went on to explain that there were many houses of worship in Tuscany that had fallen into disrepair or disuse. The Catholic Diocese had begun putting the abandoned churches on the market, although this particular one was owned privately. We walked out through the walled garden and into a white stone entry marked by a simple cross. A remarkable room with faded robin's-egg-blue walls and soaring twenty-foot ceilings opened up before us, light streaming through a broken windowpane high above double wooden entry doors. A choir loft in the center of the narthex, with a fresco featuring musical instruments that was still faintly visible, stood watch over the baptistery's stone font and wormy wooden cover. Two indigo-blue confessionals, one dating from the 1700s and the other from the 1800s, with two stone altars on either side of the nave of the church, were in good condition considering they had not hosted a priest or a confession for over thirty years.

The church was in a state of complete and utter neglect, filled with a dazzling collection of debris, bird droppings, and trash. A ladder rested precariously against the choir loft, filled with dusty, raffia-entwined wine bottles. The area where the main altar once stood had been stripped bare and consisted simply of a cement base. Two narrow arched doorways on either side of the altar led to a well-proportioned room that had formerly served as the sacristy, the room where the clergy kept their vestments. A white porcelain stove and an armoire with one door hanging forlornly from its hinge made walking through the sacristy impossible. Hunks of lard swung from the rafters, and birds had built a comfortable nest in the corner near the window.

Any sane person would have beaten a hasty retreat to the nearest exit, if there had been one available. I can't explain what happened when I saw the church, but there was a magical feel to the place that drew me in and begged me to return it to its former glory. I could see that Betsy felt it too, and I looked at Marinella with a sense of amazement and terror. What made her think that I would be interested in—or capable of—taking on a renovation project like this? After all, we had only met that morning. Yet, in that moment, with sunlight streaming through the filthy window of the sadly neglected building, I had a glimpse of what it could be, and suddenly a phrase from an e. e. cummings poem ran through my head: "i am a little church (no great cathedral.) . . . welcoming humbly His light and proudly His darkness. . . . [3]"

LET'S MAKE THEM AN OFFER
THEY CAN'T REFUSE

I couldn't have been a more unlikely prospect to take on this project. I had no design experience, with the exception of inheriting a penchant for reading interior design magazines from my mom. She would pore over back issues of *Better Homes & Gardens* and *Southern Living* and bought only the best pieces by Baker and Thomasville for our tiny two bedroom, one bath on the busy main street of Alton, Illinois. But once my mind was made up, I enthusiastically laid out the pros of the property to Chuck: good price and location, tons of potential, pretty views, neighbors always there to watch over things, unique challenge. I blissfully glossed over the cons, including the fact that he and I would soon have a starring role in the Italian version of *The Money Pit*.

The two brothers who owned the church, one of whom was still in residence upstairs, hadn't spoken to each other in several years. In addition to separating all the utilities, a new entrance to the apartment would need to be created, since no self-respecting Italian would share these with someone who was not related to them. The church needed a new roof, lighting, plumbing, heat, and a bathroom. The backyard was overgrown, and there was the obvious issue of the "dancing teacup" kitchen tiles to overcome. In spite of these formidable issues, in October of 2000, we decided to make an offer.

In Italy, there is a three-tiered system for purchasing property.

Step One: Make an offer about the same as the asking price. If the offer is too low, it might be insulting to the seller. You will be invited to take a long *passeggiata*, a slow-paced stroll taken during the early evening by Italians juggling a gelato in one hand while speaking on their cell phones with the other. I headed back to the States, assuming we didn't have a chance of our offer being accepted. Instead, approval came quickly without any counteroffer, a sure indication that we were paying too much or the owner was ecstatic anyone had made a bid for it at all. In this case, it was probably both.

I flew back to Italy in order to sign the *proposta*, an agreement confirming my intent to purchase the property, accompanied by a deposit. Sue's husband Fabio arranged for a childhood friend with offices in Florence, an attorney with a specialization known as a *notaio*, to handle the legal work. Notaios are highly respected professionals, far different from the notaries in America who simply put a stamp and date on your signature, and it's not uncommon for the buyer and seller to use the same one. The seller's presence is not required, but you must have a translator to explain the process if you are not fluent in Italian to ensure you understand all the conditions of the *contratto*. During the tedious task of reading aloud each paragraph, the purchaser is forbidden to catch up on emails or flip through juicy gossip magazines. Sue and Fabio accompanied me to the meeting and did their best to translate, and I trusted their judgment, relying on them to represent my best interests. If you don't have someone like them helping with a real estate purchase in Italy, don't even think about buying property there. These two brought a whole new level of meaning to Carole King's classic "You've Got a Friend."

There was very little communication from the seller after the proposta was signed. Although a date and time had been firmly set by the notaio for the next meeting, the seller had not confirmed that he would be attending. There was no explanation for this behavior, and, after repeated attempts by the notaio's office to contact him, we all doubted the sale would go forward. I was experiencing a wave of mixed emotions that morning, ranging from despair to relief. Fear of the potential costs and construction problems ahead had already caused a few mild panic attacks, and I was feeling a distinct lack of confidence that I could handle it all. I was just about to leave my hotel room in search of a long lunch and a glass of wine when Sue called. "He's on his way," she explained. "Are you coming or not?" I admit that I hesitated, thinking this was my last chance for a graceful exit, but I finally replied, "I'll see you there."

The seller greeted me with a warm handshake as I settled in at the conference table across from him in the notaio's office. Short and stocky, with curly brown hair and intelligent blue eyes, he politely inquired when my husband would be joining us. This was my first introduction to one of the basic facts of Italian life. Male chauvinism is alive and well, and it was inconceivable that a woman would be buying property on her own. (Chuck and I had decided, since I would be spending the most time there, that only my name should be on the contract.) Congratulations were exchanged while the seller signed documents, simultaneously trying to hide his disbelief that he was dealing solely with an American female. In a valiant effort to be chivalrous, he extended an invitation to dinner at his home in Greve that evening.

It had been a long day, and I wasn't feeling well, but it would have been extremely rude to beg off. The ever-ready chauffeurs and translators, Fabio and Sue, picked me up at my hotel in Florence, and we began the drive in a blinding thunderstorm. We know each other so well that Sue didn't even ask if I would like to sit in front. I get carsick on winding roads, so she automatically moved to the back, graciously ceding the front passenger seat. Fabio is an expert at negotiating the twists and turns of the two-lane Chiantigiana Road. But that night, exhausted and sick, it seemed as if each turn required a stop while I threw up on the side of the road. We soldiered on to the seller's remote farmhouse on the southern edge of town, and I tried to enjoy the delightful meal cooked on an open fire in their rustic kitchen. Handmade sausages, pecorino cheese, and olives were served as appetizers, followed by a pasta with pesto entrée. The seller's wife dutifully asked him to sample a ribbon of fettuccine straight from the pot to ensure his approval that it was cooked *al dente*. Roasted chicken followed, and then a dessert of panna cotta. Le Convertoie wine was served with every course, and I learned a lot about the history of my future home that evening in between trips to *la toilette*.

Step Two: A lengthy period for surveying is required by a *geometra*, (engineer) after the contratto is signed. This step in our purchase process was extended for months because the property was divided up and owned by the two brothers and their wives. Marinella served as agent extraordinaire and chief negotiator between the families, and I spent the time back in Florida dreaming about the miraculous renovation I would achieve, reassuring myself that I had made the right decision, and trying to learn some basic Italian by listening to Rosetta Stone CDs. I pored over interior design magazines in search of ideas that would guide me in decorating the old church. It's astonishing how many places of worship, both in the States and abroad, have been converted for residential use, yet so many more with incredible potential stand forlorn and abandoned.

Finally, the geometra's survey was complete, and we were ready for phase two in the process, the signing of a written contract known as a *compromesso*. Another interminable visit to the notaio's office followed, with a deposit of 10 percent of the cost of the apartment and church required. At that point, Italy had not yet joined the European Union and was using the lire as their currency. After their conversion to the euro, there were a lot of jokes at my expense about how the sale took so long the country changed its currency during the process. There is no going back after this step unless you want to kiss your deposit *arrivederci*. Compromesso seemed like a good term to me during this segment, since it took so long that the seller, fearing we would give up in spite of the initial deposit, agreed to let us live in the apartment rent-free. This offer required a leap of faith on his part, since squatters' rights rule in Italy, and it would have taken centuries to oust us if we hadn't bought the property.

Step Three: By the time the final *atto* (deed) was signed, we had moved a few necessities into the apartment and were referring to ourselves as official owners of a home in Tuscany. The challenges of trying to establish gas, Internet, and phone service, as well as an account with the power company, Italy ENEL, were overwhelming. Signing up for any or all of these services required showing up in person with an interpreter, along with my *codice fiscale* card and a cash deposit. The codice fiscale is much like America's social security number and is necessary for property purchases, opening bank accounts, setting up utilities—basically everything that is important to Italians in life. It took several tries with each utility before we actually got the service, but the process is not much different in the States.

Chuck accompanied me to Italy for the final signing in the fall of 2002, and the meeting was set at the notaio's office on a brilliant, sunny day in October. It had taken almost two years to get to this point, and we were excited to become the proud owners of a home in Greve that already seemed like ours. Chuck and I met in college and had been married for several decades at that point. He is calm, cool, and collected in every situation, in stark contrast to my short-attention-span, charge-ahead-at-all-costs approach to life. Just as I didn't know how I could see the light at the end of the tunnel at Le Convertoie, I never understood why he supported this real estate purchase. He had seen the apartment and church and grasped what needed to be done, yet we still stayed married. I offered to get a pillow made for him with the inscription, "If I were you, I would have divorced me by now." And we were just getting started.

On the morning of the closing, I received a frantic call from the usually unflappable Sue, telling me there had been a last-minute demand from the seller that would complicate matters considerably. I had met Sue in 1969 while we were going through freshman sorority rush at the University of Florida, and we'd discovered we had grown up within fifty miles of each other in Centralia and Alton, Illinois, respectively. We both pledged Tri Delta, roomed together, and remained close after graduation. Tall, slim, and blond with deep blue eyes, Sue is extremely smart, stylish, and sarcastic, with a distinctive walk we nicknamed "the Scranton shuffle." Sue moved to Italy in the 1970s after meeting her future husband, Fabio, on a study abroad program in Florence. She started her career as assistant director at Florida State's Florentine office and worked her way up to director, a position she held for many years. She deftly managed the students, their class schedules, and visiting professors while fielding calls from stateside helicopter parents. She spent countless hours at the hospital serving as a translator and resident Florentine mamma for students who overindulged, tripped on the cobblestone streets, or experienced much more serious problems.

I knew things were bad when I heard Sue's shaky voice on the other end of the line the morning of the final signing. "The seller has asked that you deposit the final funds from the sale into his account in Switzerland," Sue said.

I replied I would be happy to do that if he would bring his account information to the closing.

"That's not what he is asking of you," she explained. "He wants you to bring the cash to the closing and take a train to Switzerland, personally accompanying his wife to their Swiss bank in Geneva."

A slow burn started in the pit of my stomach, and a vision of me boarding a train covertly carrying a ton of cash in a North Face backpack flashed before my eyes. I calmly queried what the backup plan was.

"Unless you want the whole deal to implode or pay him a lot more money to cover the taxes, the sale won't go through," Sue stated, in her usual blunt manner.

There is an Italian saying, *un agnello tra lupi* (a lamb among wolves), which is particularly accurate when describing the process of being a foreigner buying property there. It had taken us two years to get this far, and when I explained the astonishing last-minute demand to him, Chuck carefully considered the situation before responding. He rarely loses his temper, playing the thoughtful foil to my overly dramatic persona. I was a (mostly) brunette version of Mount Vesuvius, ready to blow at any moment. Maybe the Mediterranean temperament was rubbing off on me, but it had little effect on him. His career in private equity had honed his skills as a silent, intent listener looking for a chink in the armor of the guys on the other side of the table. Chuck called Sue back and asked her to arrange a private meeting between him and the seller.

The meeting was set for later that morning, and Sue placed herself strategically between the seller and Chuck on her office sofa, while I took the chair at her desk. I had never seen Sue's negotiating powers in full gear before. She's not an attorney, although she has that same methodical way of working through problems that she honed through her graduate studies in Latin, ethics, and religion. In stark contrast to her zeal for knowledge, I excelled at party planning and habitually slept through my early morning physical science class, flunking the course twice.

At the meeting, serving as a mediator and psychologist (mostly for me—I was white as a sheet), Sue guided Chuck and the seller through a deal that cut me out of the train ride to Switzerland, but secured Le Convertoie's sale to us. Simply put, if Chuck had not been there, we never would have closed on the property. He was ready to walk, and the seller knew it. Sue served a key role as translator and facilitator, but this was a high stakes men's only poker game, Italian-style. We agreed to pay a higher price to include the taxes, everyone breathed a sigh of relief, and the closing went on as scheduled.

Then it was on to the bank—*andiamo!* I withdrew a huge amount of money (which had been approved ahead of time by my diligent banker), stuffing thousands of euros into a giant Prada shopping bag, also provided by my banker. As a security precaution, we called a cab to transport us to the notaio's office instead of making the twenty-minute walk. I laughed hysterically as the three of us hopped into the back of the taxi, while snapping pictures of the stash of euros I was about to turn over. We were at the point of no return.

Gathering for the final document signing, the tradition of interminable readings continued, albeit with less enthusiastic efforts at translation now that I spoke some rudimentary Italian. Suddenly, the notaio was called out of the conference room to take an important call. There were some lifted eyebrows around the table and glances toward the Prada bag, signaling it was time to pay the piper. The seller had wisely worn a dark green Barbour hunting jacket, an upper-class British weatherproof classic popular with Italians, and he hastily stuffed the coat's inside pockets with cash. The notaio returned, handshakes were exchanged, and I was officially the proud owner of an apartment and an old church in Greve.

As a final caveat on departure, the notaio mentioned that, as Le Convertoie was a historic property, we were required to open it to the public once a year. Chuck and I pictured hordes of strangers ringing the bell and trooping through our property.

"What day do we need to do that and how do we let people know?" asked Chuck.

The notaio laughed heartily and replied, "There is no law requiring you to advertise the opening on any specific day, so this is a moot point."

Benvenuto in Italia . . .

CERCA TROVA

Seek and ye shall find . . .
 I had found my Italian dream home, and now it was time to hire the professionals who would help me fulfill those dreams.

The first logical step was finding an architect. We had researched the background of our church and learned that la Chiesa di San Silvestro alle Convertoie had been named in honor of Saint Sylvester, who served as pope from 314–335. The village had been a way station for crusaders and religious pilgrims from the eleventh to the fifteenth centuries, as well as an ammunition storage site during the destructive Aragonese invasion of Chianti in 1478. The hamlet was an important producer of grain in the Middle Ages, a fortified castle surrounded by a series of small farms. In 1260, there were approximately 250 people living near the fortress, making it one of the largest settlements in the Chianti region at the time. 1260 is also the year of the bloody battle that was fought between the Sienese and Florentine armies. (Nearly eight hundred years later, citizens of both cities still regard each other with suspicion.) Florentine forces marched through Greve on their way to Monteaperti, a tiny town near Siena, today just an hour's drive away, over an old wooden bridge that still exists just below Le Convertoie.

If I'd been looking for a property to renovate in the cultural crosshairs of history, I had found it. Such an incredible property was worthy of an extraordinary renovation, and it was crucial that we hire the right architect to restore it to the standard it deserved. There is very little new construction in Italy. Architects are accustomed to redesigning and renovating older homes, so I had a large field of professionals to choose from. I outlined three criteria for the position. They must speak fluent English and share a vision for the church of restoring it to its original beauty and keeping the integrity of the structure intact. Finally, no male chauvinists need apply, since I would be dealing with the construction process almost exclusively by myself.

The first architect I interviewed was in his early forties, spoke flawless English, and taught architecture at an American university. Chuck was in town for this interview, and *Numero Uno* graciously showed us several houses in Tuscany he had renovated that were nice but not extraordinary. He lost the opportunity to work with us when Marinella called to say that he had brought his family and friends to Le Convertoie on a Sunday afternoon after we had gone back to Florida, expecting her to open it up so they could see his next project. Unfortunately, I had not hired him yet.

My second interview was with an architect who was a native of Greve. He assumed he would get the job since he had an "in" with the local officials and contractors. Stocky and gruff and appropriately decked out in a sleeveless white-ribbed "wife beater" T-shirt, he committed the cardinal sin of asking where my husband was. When I explained he would be working with me, he shrugged and mumbled the ubiquitous Tuscan term *beh*—which covers a lot of ground in Italian but roughly translated means "What the hell?"—and then headed out to the parking lot to take a cell phone call.

In a beautiful coffee table book, *Restoring a Home in Italy*, written by Elizabeth Helman Minchilli,[4] I pored over a story about a farmhouse near Siena renovated by an architect named Marco Vidotto. The house had clean lines and showed an attention to detail that I appreciated. When I emailed Vidotto, he replied in English, saying that it was his week for churches since he had just been interviewed to design a Catholic church in the heart of Siena. We scheduled a walk-through for the following week.

Blond and trim with a chiseled chin and smartly dressed, Vidotto strolled around the property with a decisive strut, hands behind his back. His blue-gray eyes widened considerably when he saw the ruin, but he was clearly intrigued by the challenge. He had the self-assurance and skills required, agreeing our church should receive the same level of respect a larger cathedral would demand.

Vidotto had an easy sense of humor—a must for working with me on this project—and never once asked when my husband would be joining us. He got the job after submitting a detailed proposal and budget, something the other two architects had failed to do. My gut reaction was that he would be an intelligent, talented, and fair partner in the project, and I was absolutely correct. Over the three years we worked together, in spite of planning and construction challenges that would have made anyone else quit in disgust, Vidotto stuck with it and even stepped up to serve as chief contractor. We ended up way over the initial budget, through no fault of his because of all the construction challenges encountered, but the final result was spectacular—thanks to Marco Vidotto.

Vidotto arranged for me to tour the house featured in *Restoring a Home in Italy* a few months later. The owner, a former fashion designer from Milan, graciously welcomed me to her renovated farmhouse overlooking the picture-perfect countryside outside of Siena. The two-story entry loggia, with its series of brick archways, stood defiantly against the blue Tuscan sky with views that stretched for miles in every direction. The owner described the long process of procuring permission to add the unusual loggia, which Vidotto had to prove to bureaucratic officials had existed previously. She lived in a hayloft on the property without running water or electricity for nearly three years during construction. The interior of the house was warm in hues of peach, terracotta, and moss green, suiting its elegant owner to a T. If I hadn't already been convinced that Vidotto was a perfect fit for Le Convertoie, I certainly was after my visit to her beautiful home.

In addition to a talented architect, I needed a top-notch interior designer to bring our church back to life. Italy, of course, has talented designers who speak English, but I wanted to work with Susan Schuyler Smith, president of Spectrum Interior Design in Vero Beach, Florida. Susan is a longtime friend, and Spectrum was a client of my public relations firm that specialized in interior design, architecture, and real estate in Vero. A blue-eyed blond with impeccable taste,

Susan was enthusiastic about the project from the inception. As soon as she arrived at Le Convertoie, she surveyed the carnage, rolled up her sleeves, and started sketching out ideas, usually while under an umbrella.

After a career in design PR, I should have thought of before and after photos, but I was knee-deep in the permitting process. Susan knew instinctively that photos would be beneficial for their historical value and to document our efforts to conserve the church. She invited her friend and noted architectural photographer, Kim Sargent, to visit while he and his wife, Joan, were on a shoot for *Architectural Digest* in northern Italy. Joan ran the idea of a "before and after" shoot by the magazine's editor-in-chief, Paige Rense Noland, and was given an okay to take exploratory photos. *AD* is arguably the most prestigious interior design magazine in the world, and you have a better chance of getting hit by lighting than you do getting a feature article in that publication. It was worth a shot, though.

I refer to this phase of the renovation as *cerca trova* (seek and you shall find), since I was looking for talented allies. That term also has special significance because Maurizio Seracini is a friend of ours and the long-time significant other of my college friend Lou. They are a stylish couple: Lou is a Brooke Shields lookalike who has carved out a career at the SACI school for design and art in Florence, and Maurizio a renowned Florentine-based art diagnostician. Maurizio discovered the phrase "cerca trova" painted on a soldier's battle flag in a corner of a fresco by sixteenth-century artist Giorgio Vasari, in Florence's Palazzo Vecchio. Vasari seemed to be enticing viewers to look further to a painting underneath his masterpiece painted in 1567.

Years of research, including X-ray scans of the Vasari, led Maurizio to believe that Leonardo da Vinci's vanished mural, *The Battle of Anghiari*, is hidden behind Vasari's work. Maurizio's quest caught the attention of CBS's Morley Safer resulting in a *60 Minutes*[5] interview in 2008, and author Dan Brown used *cerca trova* as the starting point of his blockbuster novel, *The Da Vinci Code*.[6]

In 2012, after years of petitioning the Italian government, Maurizio was allowed to investigate the Vasari painting in depth, a drama documented by *National Geographic*. Critics questioned his methodology and motives, since Vasari is a revered Tuscan artist in his own right. For preservation purposes, Maurizio was only allowed to drill twelve holes into the Vasari fresco. He is still waiting for permission to try again, although he found evidence of another type of paint at one of the drill points, a teasing reminder that his theory may be true. Italians use the word *destino* to describe this doggedly determined personal quest, but politics and economics have rendered nearly impossible Maurizio's attempts to discover if *The Battle of Anghiari* is hidden beneath the Vasari painting.

It was important to us that our church stay true to its original character, and author and historian Dario Castagno, whom we met through a mutual friend, was a crucial link for that research. Born in England, Dario speaks with a distinctively upper crust accent, but his heart is firmly planted in the Chianti region. Dario has an obsession with all things Tuscan, particularly history and red wine. He's written several books, including a humorous account of his career as a tour guide entitled *Too Much Tuscan Sun*.[7] With blond hair and perpetually dressed in faded, torn jeans and a scarf,

Dario cuts a dashing figure as he bikes, hikes, and lectures his way through the region.

Dario's connections with a famed Italian professor led to the publication of an academic treatise on our church.[8] The professor is a highly respected lecturer and author specializing in Tuscan history, and he was delighted to tour Le Convertoie. A price was agreed upon, and Dario served as translator for the text from Italian to English. The professor was so enthusiastic that he asked permission to hold a seminar for his students and colleagues in the church after his work was completed.

Translating technical architectural terms from Italian to English makes for some very stilted text. For example, "On the top left part of the façade stands out a rough granite stone in which a cross is carved, probably a sign to advise pilgrims and depraved vagabonds that assistance was granted within the church." The professor confirmed what had been found as we peeled back the layers of the church (as Vidotto had once described the process). Some of the material of the church's walls had been reused and dated back to the sixteenth and seventeenth centuries.

Various architectural styles had been added over the years, with a final renovation completed in 1848. Le Convertoie's rector at that point, Luigi Capanni, described the choir stall as "decorated with a still life painting of musical instruments, including a lyre, a flute, two horns, and four trumpets, which were tied together by a ribbon and musical manuscript." The church's upgrade was funded by the sale of food produced on the farm, and Rector Capanni, who lived in the vicarage on the grounds, was quite specific about the amount owed to the parish: eighty bushels of wheat, one bushel of fava beans, seven bushels of corn, two bushels of beans, forty-eight barrels of wine, and ten barrels of oil.

The professor discovered that several important works of art had once been in the church; these were now on display in the parish church of Santa Croce and the Museum of Sacred Art in Greve. They included a white terracotta plaque depicting the Virgin Mary and Baby Jesus from the Della Robbia school, a seventeenth-century carved painted cross and chalice, and a brass crucifix from the eighteenth century. One of the most amazing relics in the local museum is a stained glass window depicting Le Convertoie's patron saint, Pope San Silvestro, that is believed to be from the original church and designed by Francesco Granacci in the fourteenth century.

Excited about the prospect of publishing his findings, the professor neglected to ask for our approval on the number of brochures to be printed or the printing costs. His casual email to me requesting an astonishing amount of money after the fact was firmly rejected. After some heated negotiations, we received ten copies, parted on poor terms, and the professor held his seminar on Le Convertoie at another venue in the Greve area.

In my early days in Greve, finding a handyman, electrician, or furniture mover was challenging thanks to my limited language skills. I often asked Sue's husband Fabio for help with on-site translations. His salt-and-pepper hair and beard give him a distinguished air, and he speaks English with a delightful, lilting Italian accent. Fabio was an English teacher early in his career, but as an insurance representative for several of the high-end jewelry stores on the Ponte Vecchio, his schedule allowed him to drive out to Greve occasionally.

Fabio and Sue met in Florence and married around the same time as Chuck and I had in the early 1970s. They tried to carve out a life in the States, first in St. Louis near Sue's family and eventually moving to Atlanta and staying with us. Chuck and I would return home at the end of a hard day at work in Atlanta to a delicious, home-cooked meal made by Sue with wine served by Fabio, a waiter's towel draped over his shoulder for greater dramatic effect. We were heartbroken when they both found employment at the Italian Embassy in Georgia and moved into their own apartment, but we were devastated when they decided to return to live in Italy permanently a year later.

Installing a TV antenna on the old tile roof was a high priority, as the four basic Italian cable TV channels left a lot to be desired, and I hired two highly recommended local technicians. Fabio, on duty as usual, described what we needed, but the dazzling duo struggled with every aspect of the job. The minutes stretched into hours as they consulted manuals and wrestled with wires. They left to retrieve a ladder they'd forgotten to bring, then returned with wine on their breath and without the ladder. "Dumb" and "Dumber," as Fabio and I affectionately began to refer to them, spent nearly five hours at the apartment and never actually installed the TV antenna.

It wasn't all work and no play, and every Italian has a favorite bar where they stop by on a daily basis to enjoy a coffee and people watch. I found my spot, an entertaining establishment in Greve, located across from the COOP grocery store on Viale Vittorio Veneto. The proprietors' marriage was long past its expiration date and strained to the max from working side-by-side 24/7. As you enter the cafe, the first item of interest is the clock perched prominently above the glowing gold-plated Gaggia coffee machine. The clock's face, adorned by a bull and a cow enjoying a rapturous moment, represents an activity unlikely to be recreated anytime soon by this happy couple. Underneath the clock hangs a laminated copy of a hammer and a set of steel balls with a red line through it. If there is any busting of balls going on, it's going to be by the wife, who spends most of her day out on the tiny terrace chain smoking, looking bored, and apparently deaf to the calls for counter help from her hardworking soul mate. She will grudgingly appear if her husband pleads long enough, rudely grabbing the euros out of customers' hands and slamming the keys to the cash register with a cigarette hanging jauntily from her ruby-red lips.

IF THESE WALLS

COULD TALK

Historic properties in Italy are strictly protected by a government agency called La Soprintendenza per i Beni Architettonici, blessedly shortened to Le Belle Arti. Staffed by highly respected architects and historians, the agency closely monitors renovation plans and construction progress. As with everything in our newly adopted country, it is all about who you know. Luckily, Vidotto was well connected at the agency, and it was always our intention to restore the property as closely as possible to its original state. The need for modern lighting, plumbing, and heating presented a unique challenge in order to follow their directives, but difficulties with Le Belle Arti were surprisingly few and far between, except for the length of time it took to review and approve the plans.

The local officials from the Comune di Greve—the bureaucratic equivalent of the town hall in the States—were another matter entirely. Since Vidotto had committed the double sin of being a native of Rome now living and working in Siena, they constantly delayed the project. The comune's office was rarely open, and when it was, Vidotto often waited hours before being admitted for a scheduled appointment. He wryly commented that these officials should be admitted to the *Guinness Book of World Records* for their stalling tactics.

The initial demolition started in July 2005. The plan was to establish a source of water and electricity, demolish the interior of the sacristy and church floors, create an entry to the house from the church, erect scaffolding, and remove the existing roof. The roof would then be rebuilt, followed by the under-floor heating installation. Our goal was restoration, not innovation, and so the inside walls would be replastered, interior surfaces painted, and the decorative murals and pediment restored over the arch and the nave. The exterior required replastering and painting the walls of the loggia outside the front door but needed to remain essentially the same as it had looked hundreds of years before.

This was a ruin with twenty-foot ceilings, and the process was anything but straightforward or simple. Our only source of water came from the single spigot in the back garden. Its usage became a neighborhood concern because the well water is shared, and, particularly during the summer months, there are water shortages.

Friends ironically referred to me as *La Principessa del Parcheggio* (The Princess of the Parking Lot) since our purchase had included that area. My kingdom, however, was anything but regal. An area about half the size of a football field, it was always filled with trucks, cars, building scraps, and dogs. The exterior scaffolding to replace the roof was installed in

September 2005, and huge trucks loaded with the aluminum platforms had to negotiate the one-lane gravel track to reach the parking lot from the main road. The narrow foundation outside the church, lined with thriving rosemary bushes and adjacent to our neighbor's wine cellar, had to be avoided at all costs. When the equipment and scaffolding arrived, Le Convertoie's other residents revolted. Since we were usually thousands of miles away, and they were unable to do so face-to-face, our neighbors complained to everyone on site. The grumbling continued for two and a half years until the project was finished, and we really didn't blame them.

The *campanile* or bell tower of the church was replastered at the same time the new roof was put in place. The original bell had long since disappeared, initiating some snide remarks from visitors about *For Whom the Bell Tolls,* and was never replaced.

The interior scaffolding remained in place for over two years, and the construction crew also used it as a recreational lounge area. On more than one occasion when I was there for construction, I discovered some of the men taking a siesta and snoring loudly while precariously draped on top of the beams.

The Sicilian-owned construction company, which was based in Siena, hired only employees who were related to the owner. Uncles, cousins, brothers, and in-laws doubled as carpenters, bricklayers, drywall installation specialists, and day laborers. These men followed a nomadic lifestyle, traveling to Sicily to see their families only in August and at Christmas, while working in mainland Italy during the rest of the year.

I had very little interaction with the crew and was simply the naive *americana* who paid the bills. Rugged and solemn, they were not welcomed by our neighbors. *Meglio un morto in casa che un pisano all'uscio.* (Better a dead man in the house than someone from Pisa at the door.) This Italian saying is reflective of the suspicion with which Tuscans view even other Tuscans. Southern Italians are about as popular as a fox in the henhouse, and we knocked it out of the park as Americans renovating an old Italian church.

Not a lot of thought had been given to where or how the workers would relieve themselves on site. When construction began, there was no portable toilet provided and no facilities in the abandoned church. My neighbor emailed me asking if it was appropriate in America for men to defecate in newspapers and then hide those papers under her window. I assured her that was considered unhygienic no matter what nationality you were, and a porta potty was duly installed in the already crowded parking area. At least now when nature called, they went further afield. We then discovered that, although the workers had been rolling up their *cacca* in newspaper, the problem arose when one of the dogs ran off with it and buried it in an inconvenient spot.

The interior of the church required a skilled set of workers in addition to the regular construction crew, and Vidotto wisely hired Studio TRE based in Arezzo. Having painters, construction workers, plumbers, and electricians all there at the same time was referred to triumphantly as "the perfect storm." Studio TRE deftly handled the replastering, painting, and restoring the decorative murals. They renewed the pediment over the arch leading from the nave to the altar and restored two confessionals to their deep blue-green hue. One of the confessionals had a unique oval space where a religious portrait had originally hung, flanked in white stucco with the simple phrase "S. Maria" etched above. Every color was matched as closely as possible to the original *calce*, a lime-based stucco used in Italy in ancient and modern times. The stone, sandstone, stucco, and iron were also respectfully restored. A railing and gate leading to the baptismal font were cleaned and carefully rehung, and a matching arched area over the opposite entry was furnished with a simple church pew found in a warehouse in Pienza.

We fondly referred to three of Studio TRE's workers as "the painter ladies." Young, skilled, and charming, Elisa, Roberta, and Isabella brought the frescoes and original sky-blue color of the ceiling and walls back to life. They cheerfully worked alongside the construction crew, with the radio blasting and a friendly banter of jokes and stories constantly exchanged between them. Everyone brought lunch, roasting meats in the parking lot on a hibachi grill and dining al fresco in the backyard. On especially festive occasions, two sawhorses in the dining room were glammed up with a red-and-white-checked tablecloth. The painter ladies moved into Le Convertoie at one point in order to complete the job and avoid the daily two-hour commute each way from their hometown of Arezzo. They only stayed a week, complaining of a ghostly presence and the more down-to-earth dilemma of mice freely roaming the apartment and church, but they got the job done.

One of the biggest challenges was opening the church's corridor to the apartment. The buildings had once been connected, as evidenced by a "door to nowhere" at the end of our living room. Opening the door revealed a concrete wall that had to be demolished in order to fashion a hallway to the church. The plan was for the church to serve as our main living area, and the apartment's former living room would become a dining room. The sacristy would become an informal den, extra bedroom, and bath.

Adding plumbing, electricity, and heating to a building that dated from 1092 was a challenge, to put it mildly, but Vidotto found the project fascinating. When he thought something was boring—for example, dealing with the neighbors and the Comune di Greve officials—he made no bones about saying so. My concerns about the skeletons Vidotto assumed were buried beneath the church's floor were met with an amused roll of his eyes. Our meetings would drag on for hours while he meticulously covered every detail of the construction process. His thorough approach was admirable; then suddenly, after I had lost all concentration, he would spring the bad financial news on me. Italians do not like to discuss money. If you have to ask, you can't afford it.

Our plumber was Greve's finest, an accomplished professional with a keen sense of humor. Although I couldn't understand the technical details, we would both roll our eyes in unison (for different reasons) thinking about how much it was going to cost. LearnItalianPod.com posted an understated truth on their website from a reader regarding Italian plumbers: "Take out a loan and prepare to be patient."

I spent countless hours in my plumber's sweltering, windowless office trying to pay up, since plumbing in a medieval building presents an endless run of issues. Well into her fifties, his wife, a buxom blond perennially clad in a tight leopard top and/or zebra print mini skirt, tried her best to be accommodating. Her secretarial skills were questionable, and, while she and her husband were very honest and trustworthy, she never seemed able to find my paperwork in the endless filing cabinets that lined the barren concrete walls. The latest bill was never filed under anything that made sense, so a furtive call was made to The Man Himself to determine the amount owed off the top of his head. If I paid cash, I got a special discount and got out of the office faster.

Not surprisingly, unusual and unpleasant situations aside from plumbing issues arose on a regular basis. Vidotto commented, "Working on this church is like peeling back the layers of a Faberge egg." This made the construction process both fascinating and expensive as the ancient wall was stripped away. The thick walls had been needed originally to support the heavy stone vaulting of the interior ceiling, while shoring up and constructing a new ceiling for the corridor required considerable time and effort. The new space leading to the sacristy and church was carved out, linking it to the apartment and providing sufficient light to pass through after dark.

The lighting logistics presented some unique challenges, but Vidotto hired a specialist who installed recessed lights, both in the hallway and the church, linked to a computer panel placed in the corridor. The technology was impressive—a simple touch of a button would turn on the lights in the corridor, the church, or the sacristy. Children of the 1950s and technically challenged in general, Chuck and I used the same button to turn the lights on and off, rendering the expensive keypad a huge waste of money. In the church, a switch enabled square lights lining both sides of the nave to disappear into the walls, panels of pale-blue painted stucco closing over them when not in use. They needed to disappear because Le Belle Arti was unlikely to approve of their installation, but the result was unique and stunningly beautiful, especially at night.

Very little natural light was allowed into the church through the two existing small windows—one near the altar and the other over the door in the choir loft. Windows were designed to be smaller in older churches so that their presence would not weaken the walls, and Vidotto's solution was to add an interior glass door in front of the heavy wooden doors. This provided a secure alternative, enabling us to leave the wooden doors open while locking the glass door, and it kept bugs outside rather than in.

The arched vault leading from the nave to the altar became unstable after the roof was removed, and the wall suddenly collapsed. In the original church, this vault subdivided the nave while acting as a fire break between the two sections of the building. Vidotto's engineering solution required running steel rods from one side of the church to the other, anchoring them to the main roof. We had to apply for permission from the Belle Arti to do that, a process that took months. The first set of rods had to be reordered because they didn't fit properly, further delaying the project. But the second set fit perfectly and were nearly invisible braces for the fragile church's original framework.

The sacristy, located behind the altar area, had been added in the 1800s and was not subject to the strict Belle Arti rules. After the new roof was completed and the rustic, wood-beamed ceiling restored, the floors were resurfaced with the same pale rose-colored *cotto* pavers from the Viterbo area of Italy that had been used in the church. It turned out to be everyone's favorite room, with the installation of built-in bookcases to give it the feel of a cozy library, and a large, vaulted window overlooking the hills behind Le Convertoie and flooding the space with light.

Our upstairs neighbors took particular offense at the fact that when we took the old roof off, it left their "summer terrace" without a foundation. The terrace was quite small, with a lone plastic chair to enjoy the commanding views of the surrounding countryside, but it had served as a welcome retreat from the heat of their apartment during the blisteringly hot summer months. Vidotto fought against rebuilding it with gusto, but we overruled him and replaced it after the church's new roof was installed. I have an email dated May 24, 2006, with the subject line "The airport on your roof," and Vidotto christened the project "The Taj Mahal Terrace." It was large enough to serve as a helipad for Le Convertoie and was undoubtedly furnished with the same lone plastic chair, but it kept the peace between us.

We sincerely liked our neighbors, and our friendship grew over the years, but the relationship flowed both ways. When we purchased Le Convertoie, the electrical boxes were separated, but the sewage and water co-pay continued because of the shared well and the complex pipe system connecting the two apartments. Sue and Fabio returned from a morning at the Greve market to find our downstairs flooded with brackish water. A blockage from the dishwasher one floor above in the neighboring apartment had found a way to free itself by running through our washing machine. Ever the comedienne, Sue suggested posting a sign requesting "No Swimming in the Cantina."

In another twist on the shared utilities issue, an outside drain became blocked, bubbling over with raw sewage. A terrible stench enveloped the area and, with the neighbors out for the afternoon, Chuck could think of only one way to fix it. He popped open the top and, with an improvised bandana as a facemask, he began scooping out the sewage with a small cup. He filled up bucket after bucket, dumping the liquid waste into the forest beneath the stone wall leading up to the house. An even greater stench arose from the deep gap below, and our astonished neighbors returned to find Le Convertoie smelling like a roadside porta potty long past collection day. Quickly assessing the situation, our neighbor ran for a "snake," an iron rod that he inserted in the bubbling mess, and quickly cleared the blockage. We all slept with our windows closed for days afterwards, even in the blistering heat.

IT GROWS ON
THE CYPRESS TREES

In order to pay for a construction project of this magnitude, an Italian bank account was essential. Sue recommended Banco Desio Toscana on the Via Tornabuoni—Florence's answer to Rodeo Drive before Beverly Hills even existed—for all my financial needs. Luxury Italian brands, from Bulgari to Buccellati and Gucci to Pucci, are a magnet for wealthy shoppers on the elegant avenue, while the cobblestoned side streets are filled with unique, high-end boutiques and restaurants. Banco Desio's offices were on the third floor of a subdued, dark-stoned palazzo, and you either climbed the stairs or took an ancient birdcage elevator with a folding iron door. It was identical to the elevator in the gruesome murder scene from the Hitchcock classic *Charade*, so I always walked. An aging, dour guard kept an eye on the stairs, but he was usually on break or captivated by an Italian soap opera playing loudly on the black-and-white TV in his cubbyhole. Security was tighter upstairs, and at the bank's entrance door you pressed the bell and waited for an employee to buzz you in.

The lobby of Banco Desio features jaw-dropping ceiling frescoes, giving the place an atmosphere more akin to a museum than a financial institution, with a hushed, professional air. The cashiers are good looking, young, and elegantly attired in black suits with crisp white shirts. My personal banker, Simone, is one of the hardest working, most patient people I've ever encountered on any continent. Impeccably dressed in custom brown leather shoes (a must for the professional Italian male) and a blue tailored suit, Simone spoke no English. His frequent staccato bursts of rapid-fire Italian left me far behind in a trail of linguistic dust, but we mutually agreed on a way to communicate that usually involved a cell phone call to Sue for translation.

As I became more fluent in Italian, there were fewer calls to Sue and more jotting down figures on withdrawal slips that drew hysterical belly laughs from Simone. I had the money in the bank, but it was never clear to me how much I was allowed to withdraw. Newly instituted restrictions that the Italian government had placed on cash withdrawals were in place, and Simone was the first line of defense in this regulatory system. I was, on occasion, allowed to withdraw my max, and I would stroll out of the bank with thousands of euros in my purse. I walked purposefully to my rental car parked in an isolated area of Florence near Forte di Belvedere (site of the Kanye West and Kim Kardashian wedding extravaganza in 2014), but I never had a problem. This says a lot about my appearance; I didn't dress in expensive clothing, and I carried a cheap purse. This is a cardinal sin in Italy, since even criminals can tell when you are carrying a Gucci knockoff, but mostly I just got lucky.

Writing checks on an Italian bank account poses its own challenges. This is still a cash-heavy economy, and many Italians have blocks of checks that last for decades. The checks are in the same format as their American counterparts, requiring you to write out the amount due in script. In Italian, the numbers are written together; for example, 3,960 euros is *tremilanovecentosessanta*. In the time it took to write that out, I could have stopped at the nearest bar for an espresso. I couldn't pay cash for everything, so I practiced writing the number on a scrap of paper first, and then asked for confirmation it was done correctly.

Cash was, however, enthusiastically preferred as part of the payment process. On one hot, sticky Friday afternoon, I arrived home with a substantial amount of money due for the work completed over the past week. The head of the construction firm was not on site that day, so he asked me to give the payment to his cousin. I was concerned about this, since I had not met his cousin and, in fact, I didn't know any of the workers' names. When I questioned the wisdom of this, his reply was simply, "But, *signora*, I will kill him if he doesn't return to my office with the money." Conjuring up the famous scene from *The Godfather* when the horse's head shows up in the bed, I counted the cash over and over. At five o'clock on the dot, the cousin arrived and solemnly counted the cash. Nodding briefly and wishing me a gentle *buonasera*, he made a gallant exit with the sack of cash. I double-locked the door after his departure and could not get the movie's "Speak Softly, Love" theme song out of my head for days.

HOLY HAND JIVE!

Although I was becoming fairly fluent in construction terms, I also used the time-honored Italian tradition of hand gestures to communicate. When words and gestures failed me, pointing, grunting, jumping up and down, and acting out scenarios worked. Isabella Poggi, a professor of psychology at Roma Tre University, estimates that there are 250 gestures used in everyday Italian conversations.[9] They are an essential part of the culture and quintessentially Italian. Gestures are used for emphasis, running the gamut of every emotion: anger, appreciation, approval or disapproval, excitement, or hope. When you've had enough, *Basta!* is accompanied by a slicing hand moved back and forth at the base of your throat. There are numerous insulting and obscene gestures that are not limited to America's familiar middle finger salute, although that is also popular. Hands in prayer were appropriate considering the venue and used often by the construction crew to show, "We are hopeful, but what do you expect?"

In spite of my slow but steady linguistic progress, *piano, piano,* there were still plenty of times over the course of eleven years in Italy when I seemed to have made a recent asylum break. I acted out digging ditches, and swimming against the current. I counted out money with an evil laugh and resisted further lunch courses by pushing my stomach out and crying, "Ho, ho, ho!" In one particularly low moment, I grabbed my wine glass and hit it (gently) against my head to indicate the need for further refreshment. Desperate to get the bill—Italian waiters expect you to linger for hours before they bring you the check—I have pretended to faint and followed the workers' lead by putting my hands in a praying position, murmuring, "*Mio Dio, il conto, per favore!*"

One of the nicest offhanded compliments I received regarding my uphill battle with Italian was at an hours-long meeting with Vidotto, Studio TRE, and the electricians. After one of the participants unloaded about a problem with a slew of Italian obscenities, Vidotto remarked with a nod in my direction, "Careful! She knows a lot more Italian than you think." I was following the trash talk pretty closely and, for once, I was taking notes.

Expert skills were required to patronize an Italian language only hair salon. I began turning gray at twenty-one and needed to keep up the coloring regimen in my adopted country, so I asked Sue for a recommendation. She mentioned Hair Studio Gianluca as a popular styling stop for FSU students and faculty.

Conveniently located just steps from my bank on Via Tornabuoni, the slick salon offered color, cuts, and a neverending rotation of chic clientele. The head stylist and salon owner, Gianluca, was of Greek–Italian descent and had studied his craft in Paris, a fact he mentioned every couple of minutes. Paris's fashion scene had apparently rubbed off on Gianluca too, because whatever the season, he always wore the same haute couture. His ensemble consisted of tight black leather pants, a black leather studded jacket, black combat boots, and no shirt, his hairy chest wilting or rising according to the humidity and temperature.

Although clearly a styling genius, he often lost all sense of time and place, falling hopelessly behind in his schedule. His tall, blond Swedish receptionist tried valiantly to keep Gianluca on track, but even she could not tame the flirtatious hairdresser. Appointments for a color and cut evolved into a four- or five-hour ordeal, as the master would greet, color, cut, and highlight his way in and out of the salon, often disappearing for hours at a time. Rock music blasting and his battery mysteriously recharged, he would reappear, look disoriented, then recommend a crimson-streaked updo for my next visit.

No matter how many Italian classes I took, I rarely understood a word my neighbors said. I froze in fear when they asked me to sit and talk, have a coffee, or discuss the latest sewage problem. That wasn't because I didn't enjoy their company, but in 90 percent of our conversations, I was completely clueless about what we were discussing. I caught a phrase here and there, but their fast-paced Tuscan dialect was like Greek to me. My linguistic inabilities caused me to nod idiotically and answer, *Si, si,* or *Alora* (Well then!) My favorite response was *C'è sempre qualcosa* (It's always something), thrown in to show empathy about an illness or during discussions on the challenges of raising children. Important topics such as, "We will soon be out of water," or

"It's your turn to pay the gas bill," required a phone-a-friend to confirm what I thought I had heard.

In one particularly humiliating incident, my designer Susan and I watched in astonishment as a baby owl fell off the newly tiled roof, landing in the parking lot. Worried that the neighbor's dogs would make quick work of it, Susan scooped it up and took it into our back yard. She gently placed the tiny owl in a corner of the garden, and I ran upstairs to ask our neighbor if there was something we could do to help it. I was reduced to hooting and making round circles around my eyes as I explained our predicament. Clearly intrigued and with a twinkle in his eye, he followed me downstairs, where I again began to pantomime the situation. It was a primitive form of charades at best, but he seemed to get the picture. Unfortunately, when I took him over to show him the poor creature, it was nowhere to be found. In our excitement, Susan and I had missed the fact that either the baby had flown away or the mother had come back and retrieved it. Chuckling to himself, my ever-patient neighbor returned to the relative safety of his own apartment.

I turned the tables when our neighbors were rendered speechless by the stark difference between the life of dogs in Italy and America. Their dogs, born and bred to be roaming guard dogs, did just that. Spaying and neutering are not part of country culture and, unless you're a pug, the favorite breed of Italian city dwellers, you dine on table scraps and sleep in the yard. The dogs are truly loved and valued, but they are not coddled. One sunny Sunday, I welcomed our upstairs neighbors for a home-cooked meal at our house—a first. They looked skeptical as they entered the kitchen, as Sunday lunch is the most important meal of the week. Their relief was obvious when they realized Sue and Fabio would also be guests, as this meant on-site translators and that Sue was at least cooking the pasta. Chatting amicably, they noticed a photo of our handsome black-and-white English springer spaniel taped to the refrigerator. Bentley was enjoying a trip around a swimming pool on a giant plastic swan float. Their jaws dropped as they took in the scene, and I don't think they would have been any more surprised if Bentley had been balancing a cocktail with a tiny umbrella in it and dressed in a tux and tails.

Susan played her own game of "hand jive" when I decided to redo the kitchen. With renovations close to being finished on the church, I realized that the kitchen's outdated décor made it pale in comparison to the beautiful rooms just next door. I hadn't thought of myself as a serial renovator, but after putting all that time and effort into the church, neglecting the kitchen (and subsequently the master bath) seemed ridiculous. I didn't tell my husband or architect about my brilliant plan, but instead turned to Susan for help. (To be honest, I didn't want Chuck to know how much it was going to cost, and I felt Vidotto would be bored handling a kitchen redo.)

Florence is home to some of the greatest artisans in the world, and the superb kitchen store, Marche Cucine, has showrooms in the city center. The store is laid out in vignettes illustrating the rustic Italian appeal of the company's design products, and Susan and I hoped we could point, grunt, and order an entire room there within a couple of hours. Our appointment started at ten and ended around four, when I had a meltdown due to a lack of food and drink. I left Susan to soldier on, earning her the nickname of the "Energizer

Bunny." She designed, sketched, and somehow purchased all the necessary cabinets, appliances, and hardware needed to refit my country kitchen without speaking a word of Italian with the Marche Cucine staff, who spoke no English. Meanwhile, I enjoyed a refreshing and restorative glass of *vino rosso* at a nearby bar.

Nothing is easy in Italy, and the kitchen renovation proved to be a lot more complicated than the initial eight hours at the design center indicated. In spite of several on-site visits by a design team to measure, the cabinets arrived and didn't fit, while the entire floor had to be pulled up and refitted to accommodate the new kitchen island. We had also missed the fact that Marche Cucine would not be supplying the labor for the project, so we had to pull men off the church restoration to help. The light fixture company's chief broke his leg skiing, inexplicably holding up the project for weeks. It was off to the confessional again for me, and Vidotto was furious when he had to be called in for help at a very late hour.

Acting out scenarios isn't limited to English-speaking visitors; Italians do it sometimes, too. Chuck developed an abscessed tooth on one visit, with the left side of his face swelling up to "Alvin and the Chipmunks" proportions. Since we weren't heading back to the States for several days, we called the local dentist for an appointment. The walls of the grim waiting room were decorated with ancient rusting dental tools, and I attempted to lighten the somber atmosphere by describing how they would soon be used. (I stepped over the line by mentioning a scene from the Dustin Hoffman classic, *Marathon Man*.) Focusing on understanding the results after the dentist completed the X-rays, I couldn't understand a word he said. This was a matter of some importance to Chuck so, as usual, I called Sue for translation reinforcements. Although she had spent forty years in Italy, she couldn't understand him either. The dentist pretended to pull out the tooth, howling in pain, eyes wide in terror, then wrote out a prescription for an antibiotic and sent us on our way.

Thanks to language and cultural misunderstandings, I found ways to look silly on a daily basis and Sue, never one to sugarcoat things, would simply comment, "Get over it, Kyle."

I quickly learned to drive like a bat out of hell, as my adopted countrymen did, and communicated on the road by shifting into sixth gear and moving on or pulling over to let them pass. Driving is a passion for all Italians, and no one in Greve seemed to enjoy his job more than the local mailman. *Il signore delle poste* began honking as soon as he started down the steep, one-lane road toward Le Convertoie. Meeting another vehicle, he cheerfully slammed his tiny Fiat into reverse and backed up the hill at breakneck speed. As skilled as a member of a crack Daytona 500 team, he whipped the car aside to make room for other vehicles—mere inches from an olive tree trunk, sideways into a ditch, or even backing half a mile up onto the highway. With a tip of his hat and a huge grin, he would grind his car back into first gear and speedily continue on his appointed rounds.

I usually drove when friends were in Italy but, occasionally, circumstances dictated a designated driver. La Castellana in Montefioralle is a Slow Food Movement restaurant, a family-owned gem where heavenly pasta with truffles and local wines are served. At one memorable Sunday lunch there, Betsy, Susan, and I were invited by a jolly group of Italians to join their table. We had no trouble understanding each other in spite of the language barrier and grew boisterous as our meal was followed by glasses of limoncello, a lemon-laced after-dinner liqueur. After the limoncello came a variety of colorful and potent *grappas*, a flavored grain alcohol. If you are drinking grappa after having wine with lunch and a limoncello to follow, God have mercy on you.

I had enjoyed myself thoroughly and was not in top driving form, so the non-imbibing Susan took the wheel. Unfortunately, it had been years since she had driven a stick shift. Sympathetic observers quickly gathered as she struggled to free the rental car from the parking spot I had carved out over a huge tree trunk. (Parking is scarce in Montefioralle.) Shifting from reverse to first and back again, Susan finally extricated the vehicle as the amazed crowd burst into applause. Lurching down the road in second gear, Susan asked what the burning smell was, and I smugly replied, "Our clutch, of course."

Since Chuck spoke very little Italian, and I always had trouble understanding our neighbors, we had some unusual meals with them that always called for a lot of nods and smiles. Chuck was enlisted to help with the Le Convertoie grape harvest early one morning with a quick knock on the door and a motion from our neighbor for my husband to follow him. He returned around five o'clock looking like something the cat dragged in and couldn't move for three days afterwards. As a thank you, we were invited for a *vendemmia* (grape harvest) celebration at their home. Sausages were grilled on the open hearth in their roomy, frescoed living room, accompanied by a heaping bowl of pasta with zucchini.

The feast continued with an unusual secondo, *uccellini*, or miniature grilled birds on a skewer. Slow roasted on a stick, their tiny beaks were wide open, appearing to chirp a final call for help after a few turns on the red-hot grill. There was no mistaking the look of amusement in our hosts' eyes as we dutifully munched on the crunchy delicacy. That night, our stomachs churned for hours, just as the uccellini had on the spit.

I sometimes got a little too confident language-wise when ordering at restaurants. Susan and I stopped for a late lunch one day at Trattoria Cibreino in Florence, owned by famed chef Fabio Picchi. Sadly, Chef Picchi passed away in March 2022. There is no printed menu and no pasta, but the divine dishes the chef creates are worth the wait in line, as there are no reservations taken.

Hoping to show off my repertoire of menu Italian, I confidently chose the collo di pollo stuffed with meat, spices, truffles and pistachios for us. When the steaming dish arrived, we were both astonished. Proudly strutting its stuff in the middle of the white porcelain dish, the fowl's neck stretched up towards heaven, a sumptuous broth circling it. To her credit, Susan ate the entrée with no complaints, but I was never allowed to order for her again without a confirmation of the dish's ingredients from the waiter. My lack of fluency never kept me from smugly noting other people's faux pas. A few of my favorite queries from visitors:

- "**Can we pay the taxi drivers in dollars?**" *Response:* "Sorry, but Italy uses the euro as their currency."

- "**When I go to an ATM, will I get dollars in return?**" *Response:* see above.

- "Why don't they have spaghetti and meatballs on the menu?" *Response:* "Take the next train to Naples." Tuscans would rather eat shrimp and grits than add meatballs to their pasta.

- "Who is 'Al Dente'? *Response:* "Al is not a person. That is the way Italians like their pasta, and it translates as 'to the bite.'"

- "Did you know there was no yodeling in Switzerland in spring?" *Response:* "I did not, and that has absolutely nothing to do with Italy."

It is admirable to try and learn a few phrases in la lingua italiana before you arrive. I found these the most useful:

- *Un'altra bottiglia di vino, per favore.* Another bottle of wine, please. (A necessity while you wait for the bill, although that will start the process all over again.)

- *Quanto velocemente stavo andando, signor carrabiniere?* How fast was I going, officer?

- *Ho bisogno di reipotecare la casa per spedirlo negli Stati Uniti?* Will I need to remortgage to ship that to the United States?

ALBERGO CALIFORNIA:
YOU CAN CHECK OUT
ANYTIME YOU LIKE,
BUT YOU CAN NEVER LEAVE

As anyone who has lived in an old house understands, you're sometimes buying into more than leaking pipes and creaking floorboards. The decorating website Houzz.com surveyed its readers asking, "Would you live in a haunted house?" After living at Le Convertoie for a while, I felt an immediate kinship with the participant who responded, "Actually, I could use the company." As our architect cheerfully noted, "There are dead bodies everywhere in Italy," and you can certainly expect that to be true if you're renovating a medieval church in Tuscany.

During the Crusades, Le Convertoie served as a place of refuge, a sanctuary, and a hospital for sick, wounded, and weary travelers on their way to and from the Holy Land. The floor of our church was tiled in pale stone, and in the center was a large cross. Bodies were routinely buried in Italian churches until the 1800s, and Vidotto was certain there was at least one skeleton underneath that cross, and probably more in the areas of the floor marked by smaller crosses. Thus, it was no surprise when the old floor was pulled up that there was not one, but a total of eight skeletons buried beneath it. One of the workers ironically announced that he had found the burial site of Saint Sylvester, the church's namesake. Interred facing the altar, the skeleton was quite tall for a man from that era and most likely the remains of the rector of the parish in the late 1700s. Seven more skeletons surfaced, this time in a shallow grave near the ancient wooden entry doors. One was very small, possibly a child curled into a fetal position near a corner—while the rest were larger, lying one atop the other. Not wishing to disturb the bodies, we placed wooden planks over the crypts, although after a couple of glasses of wine at lunch, one of the Sicilians fell in and had to be rescued by his chuckling colleagues. We were careful to install the under-floor heating system around the crypts and solemnly sealed them up with a prayer for their eternal peace (and ours, too.)

I had read the popular "brick lit" books, including *Under the Tuscan Sun*[10] and *A Year in Provence*,[11] identifying with the familiar refrain of falling in love with a ruin, struggling to learn how to live in a new culture, and learning lessons about life and love in the process. None of those books prepared me for the haunting experiences I had at Le Convertoie, the first occurring when I was visiting in August. (That's a rookie mistake—do not go to Italy in August when it's unbearably hot, there is no air conditioning, and many shops and restaurants are closed while the proprietors are at the beach.)

At dusk, I checked the windows in the apartment's living area to insure they were locked. The windows were typical of old Tuscan homes—large, arched, and heavy, opening in toward the room, not out, with locks in the middle. As I checked the last one, I felt a sudden push that sent the window straight into my forehead. I fell backwards onto the couch, which was fortunately located just below the window, but I was pushed with such force that it nearly knocked me out. Failing to come up with a reasonable explanation, I relatched the window and headed upstairs to find some Aleve.

Around three the next morning, I woke up to the sound of footsteps on the gravel path below. Le Convertoie was once a fortress, and our apartment was located at least forty feet above this narrow pathway. I listened with curiosity as phantom footsteps marched back and forth, like those of a sentry keeping watch. *Maybe it's a wild boar*, I thought hopefully. They were plentiful in our area—but the rhythmic sound of a crunching, high-stepping cadence continued. I then upped the RX from Aleve to Ambien, explaining the moral to my entire tale: "Never travel without a lot of drugs." The next morning, I checked to see if there was any trace of who or what had been parading at such a late hour on the pathway. The gravel was smooth and shiny in the early light, and there was no logical explanation whatsoever.

Soon after we purchased the property, friends from the States visited, taking pictures of the ruined church with the cement altar as a focal point. The building had been stripped of any valuable religious memorabilia years before, and there were only a few candles and Marlboro Light cigarette butts left on the altar. We returned the next day to find the candles and cigarettes eerily stacked in neat rows on top of the central cross, although the heavy double entry doors were still locked. As we examined the photo to make sure we weren't imagining things, a bird began to beat against the glass window above the entrance. Exhausted, it finally dropped to its death on the church's front porch.

One odd encounter just before Easter turned out to be a case of cultural misunderstanding. I heard a knock at the door and opened it to find an African priest in a long, black flowing cassock and white clerical collar standing before me. The Nigerian switched seamlessly into English when he realized I was American and explained he was working as a missionary in Italy, wanting only to bless our house. I politely refused since I had no idea if he was legitimate or not. I later discovered that this was a traditional visit during the Holy Season and everyone in the area welcomed the African priest, who appeared to ward off evil spirits for the following year. If only I had taken him up on his offer.

One summer evening, as I was getting ready to head to Florence, a stiff wind blew up out of nowhere, rustling the leaves on the trees in front of the apartment. The trees on either side of a ten-foot radius, however, remained strangely still. I had the same sensation I'd had so many times before that something otherworldly was watching and waiting. I threw up my hands in defeat indicating I'd had enough and ran my hand under my chin in one of the Italians' favorite rude, all-encompassing gestures. The wind suddenly stopped, and a sense of peace and calm enveloped me. I had struck a shaky bargain with the ghost of Le Convertoie, who at least seemed to have a sense of humor in addition to the nasty smoking habit.

Our ghost struggled to find a modern way to communicate, and for several months during the winter of 2005 when the house was empty, our phone automatically dialed the same number continuously between one and four in the morning. Our bill spiked, but the number called turned out to be a discontinued computer server in Siena. After months of haggling, Telecom Italia dropped the charges, and no one could ever explain what happened.

We had continuous problems with our Internet and cable service, mainly because we were living in a centuries-old building with ten-foot-thick walls. This required spending a lot of time hanging precariously over the church's front terrace trying to get service, or driving in to Greve to use the Internet café. Nicknamed *L'ufficio* (the office), Ricky Gervais or Steve Carell would have felt right at home there. A sweet, elderly gentleman would often stop by the restaurant selling pictures of Italian saints. In my wallet, I still carry the wrinkled, comforting image of Padre Pio, a Catholic friar born in the late 1800s, that I bought from the gentleman. Padre Pio's words of wisdom are good ones to live by, whether you're renovating an old church in Italy or not: "Pray, hope, and don't worry."

One of the eeriest ghostly calling cards we received came after some Italian friends hosted a Sunday lunch at Le Convertoie while we were out of town. Our property manager, Lori, noticed a cigarette burn on the box springs of the mattress of the green bedroom a few days after the party, although our friends assured us no one had stayed overnight or even gone upstairs. Lori's cell phone camera captured a perfect brown circle about four inches in diameter burrowing deep into the mattress padding. How it got there and why it didn't light the mattress on fire is still a mystery, but the thought of a smoldering fire in the house haunted us for months.

My brother and sister-in-law had two encounters with our smoking ghost while staying at Le Convertoie in that same bedroom. Ready to retire for the evening, Bonny was in bed, and Bob was just turning off the light when the mattress on his side of the bed began to sink under the weight of an unseen visitor. The temperature in the room suddenly dropped, and they felt an electric current running through the air. After what seemed like an eternity, the mattress slowly rose back up, and the temperature returned to normal. On another visit, Bob and Bonny woke to find the room filled with smoke. Tearing open the window and frantically searching the house for the source of the fire, they found no evidence of a fire in the rest of the building. Just as quickly as it had appeared, the smoke dissipated.

Final confirmation that our house was straight out of *The Haunting* central casting came during the re-landscaping of the tiny backyard garden. Neglected and overgrown, it was crying out for some tender loving care. An expat landscape designer, who lived nearby, was recommended, and I was thrilled to be working with a fellow American, expecting no linguistic misunderstandings. We agreed on a plan that included roses, fruit trees, and an irrigation system that would run off the well below our house. In hindsight, I don't know why this plan didn't set off alarm bells. It called for a watering system required to run straight up a forty-foot incline and siphon water from a well that frequently ran dry during the summer. A crew that she used regularly was hired to install the irrigation system and dig up the old garden, and since the house was unlivable at that point, I was staying at a hotel. The landscaper was on a lecture tour in the States, so it fell to her husband to oversee the project.

I got a cryptic call from Sue one evening during this process asking to meet me to discuss a grave matter. We met at a bar near her apartment in Florence, and Sue seemed very anxious. Taking a deep breath, she explained that while digging several feet down to install the irrigation system, the crew had stumbled onto an ossuary, a site where multiple skeletal remains are stacked to conserve space. The sight had been so frightening that the workers had run off, calling the landscaper's husband to report their gruesome discovery.

"How many skeletons did they find?" I asked Sue nervously.

"Hundreds," came her reply.

As I thought back on Le Convertoie's history—the battles fought nearby and the church's importance as a refuge for religious pilgrims—it was suddenly clear that quite a few of them hadn't made it past our backyard. If our architect's admonition about dead bodies all over Italy was true, we had won the skeleton lottery.

The ossuary was covered over with soil and gravel, and in a profound, prayerful moment, I decided not to dig down deep enough to confirm or deny the discovery. Vidotto had called the comune officials when we discovered the skeletons in the church, and they thanked him for the information but replied they didn't care. The church renovation had been completed, so there was no chance that reporting the discovery of an ossuary would hold up construction for years. In fact, it explained a lot!

We planted the roses, graveling over the rest of the garden, and I got stuck with a big bill for a sprinkler system that never sputtered into existence. I never discussed the discovery with our neighbors, preferring to leave Pandora's coffin firmly closed.

A view of the Borgo of Le Convertoie. The church (la chiesa di Silvestro alle Convertoie) is on the far right of the picture, the ivory-colored building with columns.

"Before" sun-streaked photo of the nave of the church under construction. Picture is facing the front door and vestibule from the altar (not shown). There are two smaller altars and two confessionals (shown with scaffolding) on either side of the church, and the cross on the floor is outlined as the floor was carefully excavated around it.

"After" photograph of the renovated nave, vestibule, baptistry, and choir loft, featuring the original frescoes. The terracotta circle in the cross on the floor marks the spot where one of the skeletons, presumably that of a parish priest, was discovered. Niches above the side altars show the painting of the priest presenting baby Jesus at the Temple (left) and, on the facing altar, "the Bishop" gazes serenely over the finished living area. Recessed lighting on either side of the church disappeared at the flip of a switch.

"Before" shot with a view of the nave and sanctuary from the front entry. The curved niche in red sits above the area where the original altar stood.

"After" photo facing the altar area from the front door. A custom oak cabinet sits in place of the altar and houses electronic equipment. An antique chest sits behind the yellow sofa.

The sacristy under construction.

The renovated sacristy area, showcasing the terracotta ceiling and beams, was furnished with an antique Italian desk and "throne" chair. Custom bookcases and a sectional sleeper sofa in a pale blue tweed continues the overall color scheme.

The dining area of the adjoining apartment, with two overstuffed chairs in a Schumacher blue and gold fabric overlooking the garden. Stairs lead up to the three bedrooms and two baths of the apartment.

The renovated kitchen, with its huge fireplace as a focal point. Oak plates and Italian Santi's (metal religious figures) rest on top of the mantle. Decorative iron andirons found at the market in Arezzo flank the hearth.

A 1700s confessional pre-renovation.

The 1700s indigo blue confessional
was restored to its original beauty.

The garden was designated to enjoy the views of the surrounding Tuscan countryside. A low maintenance gravel grounds the area with pots filled with boxwood and a pomegranate tree to define the garden. The bricked, arched entry leads into the apartment.

SLEEP TIGHT, DON'T LET
THE BEDBUGS BITE

The workers had begun tearing down a ceiling stuffed with what appeared to be ancient hay in the church when they left for one of Italy's summer holiday weekends. I settled into bed that evening and dozed off, only to wake up suddenly as I felt something slowly inching up my leg. Jumping up, I discovered that the bed was covered in tiny brown insects, slogging solemnly to and fro. I had several bites, and the area around them began to swell up and itch in an angry allergic reaction to the assault.

I threw the sheets in the washing machine and moved to another bedroom. The guest room seemed free of the creepy critters, but the next morning, I woke up to find they had switched rooms with me. I was now covered in bites and itching all over. Too large for bedbugs, the brown, blood-sucking insects stumped even the exterminator. He sprayed the mattresses with a foul vapor that left them smelling like a giant can of Raid, leaving us homeless for a month due to its toxic qualities.

I later read about a mutinous group of train passengers who pulled the emergency cord near Milan after being attacked by hordes of ticks in one of the compartments. We may have disturbed the nest of some unknown predator during the renovation, but it's more likely a visitor to Le Convertoie had plopped their infected suitcase on the bed. We had several incidents when the bugs came back, biting friends and family alike. They disappeared as mysteriously as they had arrived once the project was completed.

In another bizarre incident, I broke out in a leprosy-like rash on my hands—a hideous, oozing mass that itched and drove me crazy. Benadryl and calamine lotion could not soothe it, so in desperation, I wrapped my hands in bandages and headed down to the local farmacia. When I unveiled them for the pharmacist on call, she recoiled in horror, immediately calling for backup assistance. Everyone began chattering at once, and a plethora of creams and potions were offered. I took all of them, although the rash only disappeared after I began a course of prednisone. My theory is I was allergic to my adopted country, but the real source of the problem, diagnosed as contact dermatitis, was never determined.

Our neighbor Bianca had repeatedly warned me about scorpions, and she insisted that we always wear shoes in the house. Scorpions love old houses, and we found several lurking in the cantina and in the shower.

When windows are open on a daily basis, *insetti* (insects) enter at will. One morning, I heard a sharp cry and ran upstairs to find Betsy, who was visiting, hopping around on one foot and howling in pain. Bianca had stirred up a hornet's nest while sweeping outside, and one of them had found its way through the window. Barefooted Betsy had stepped directly on it, and the half dead hornet, its stinger still intact, was twirling merrily around in the bare sole of her foot. The wound immediately began to swell, and Betsy could barely walk for the next three days.

CASA MIA È CASA TUA

Although we welcomed friends and family, I worried constantly about potential problems arising when we weren't on site. My solution was to write a manual entitled *Enjoying Your Stay at Le Convertoie* for guests. The handy booklet, elegantly encased in a white plastic, three-ringed binder, included directions to the local dump in Greve, along with how to collect firewood without being mauled by the two large dogs that patrolled the grounds. ("Bring Pup-Peroni treats and back slowly away from your car as you generously distribute them.") Use of the gas stovetop was discouraged, but for the budding chefs who visited, knowledge of the words *aperto* and *chiuso* (open and close) on the gas valves were crucial.

Le Convertoie presented many unique challenges. Before the kitchen was renovated, the stove didn't work at all, and the heat and hot water were tricky. The hot water heater was located in the closet next to the kitchen sink, with a chronic problem of spiders building nests in the heater itself, making cold showers even in the winter months a way of life. It took quite some time for the water to heat up, even if the spiders were on vacation. You did not rinse or wash dishes in the sink while someone was taking a shower unless you had a perverse sense of humor. If the downstairs and upstairs lights were on at the same time, using a hair dryer would blow the fuse. A bird built a nest in the heating exhaust pipe in the church, died, and stopped up the pipe so the heat wouldn't go on.

We had a washer and dryer in a small room off the kitchen, but the instruction manual was, naturally, in Italian. I labeled the settings in the booklet (i.e. #1 white and pre-wash, #2 colors) but was unable to translate #7 and #9, advising visitors to stick with the *lavaggio rapido*.

The dryer, which most Italians do not have, vented out of the tiny window, and Bianca would drop by, poking her head through the window and laughing mischievously to remind me of my useless purchase. Italians rarely use dryers, preferring to hang their laundry in the yard and let it dry naturally in the sun. The drying rack in the backyard was more practical or—for bed linens and towels, unless you loved a scratchy, textured feel—the professional laundry in Greve was a better choice.

Although I discouraged their help, two couples from Florida staying at Le Convertoie dropped off their linens and towels at the professional laundry on their last day in town. None of them spoke a word of Italian, so they grabbed a small Italian–English translation guide they assumed would have the language basics included. They had no idea that the book, a prank gift from Fabio, had been used during World

War II solely for the purpose of translating commands and taking prisoners.

Dropping off the huge pile of linens, the group merrily announced the first line in Italian to the laundry attendant, "Put up your hands and drop your gun." Stunned, she put up her hands and motioned nervously that she had no weapon. "How many men are in your battalion?" Hands in the air, the attendant numbly pointed toward the owner. "That is all," they commanded, as they slowly backed out of the front door. Our friends howl with laughter every time they tell the story, but word spread quickly in Greve that a merry band of *americani* had tried to take over the local *lavanderia*.

The three pages of instructions for the TV and DVR were in the bottom drawer of a beautiful honey-colored oak dresser placed where the original altar had been. The dresser was custom-made for the space, designed by Vidotto from a picture I had seen in a magazine, and served as the focal point for the entire church. The TV system was so complicated that we recommended reading a good book and enjoying a glass of wine instead. It was sometimes possible to tune into the BBC, the Golf Channel, and college football games from the States at midnight. There were a few Italian channels owned and controlled by then Prime Minister Silvio Berlusconi, reflecting his version of Italian entertainment for the masses: slapstick game shows or risqué programs featuring scantily clad Italian "housewives."

The cardinal sin committed by guests, in addition to leaving the Internet running on our antiquated computer in the sacristy, was leaving the upstairs shutters and windows open while touring the Chianti countryside. The weather changed rapidly, and rain warped the wooden frames, allowing various species of insetti to enter (before my brother-in-law installed screens ordered from the States) or allowed the insufferable afternoon heat to waft in.

Some of my favorite visitors were "the Tilghman Clan." Betsy's husband, Jim, is the oldest of four boys born and raised in Miami. The Tilghman brothers travel as a team, and we were always happy to welcome them to Le Convertoie. Middle brother, Bob, is your basic Bob Vila of *This Old House* handyman fame and was put to work immediately fixing plumbing problems, irrigation systems, and sewage and lighting issues while on his "dream vacation" in Italy.

We had many adventures with the Tilghmans and our mutual friend, Elyta Watkins, during their visits to Italy. The most frightening occurred when we visited the Cinque Terre area of Liguria, five picturesque towns with sun-kissed, pastel houses carved into a rugged coastal region on the Italian Riviera. The region has become one of the most popular tourist destinations in the Mediterranean, overrun with visitors who hike along the spectacular coastline between the villages of Riomaggiore, Manarola, Corniglia, Vernazza, and Monterosso al Mare.

We had rented a minivan to accommodate the group, and I was at the wheel. The area is only a three-hour drive from Greve, and we were moving rapidly along the Autostrada when, suddenly, the car in the lane to our immediate left blew a tire. The deafening boom was followed by the shock of having a front row seat to observe the driver's struggle to control the vehicle. His car began to weave and sway, heading over the line and toward us to his right, then swerving wildly into the passing lane to his left.

Time seemed to stop, and the thought of being the person responsible for killing off several people of the same family in addition to Elyta, my husband, and myself flashed through my mind. I yelled at my suddenly very quiet passengers, "What do I do? What do I do?" No one responded—a first in that group—and I assumed they were stunned into silence. As the out-of-control car lurched toward us again, I downshifted from sixth to third gear and slowed the van enough to give the staggering vehicle room to swerve in front of us toward the emergency lane.

Tragedy was averted, but when we arrived at our destination in Santa Margherita, I jumped out of the van, leaving my passengers in the dust, and headed for the closest bar. I don't drink martinis, especially at lunch, but I made an exception that day.

The only other person who worked harder at Le Convertoie was my brother-in-law, Bob Baldock, who spent countless hours refinishing doors and windows. Bob and Bonny flew over to install the window screens, and he designed, ordered, and installed the wine cellar cabinets for the cantina from a company based in California. (Some things are just easier to do in English.) The cantina stayed cool and dry, filled with Tuscan wines from our travels throughout the region. Furnished with a long, wooden table found on the side of the road, a set of six ladderback chairs with straw seats, and a red-and-white checkered tablecloth and straw-covered Chianti bottles with candles, the cantina was charming and inviting if you remembered to dodge the scorpions.

LA SIGNORA BIANCA

One of my most treasured memories from Tuscany is my friendship with la signora Bianca, the elderly bread maker I met on my first visit to the property. Well into her eighties, Bianca was smart, charming, witty, and ready to chat at any hour in spite of the language barrier. She worked weekdays at Le Convertoie from sunrise to sunset. In addition to her baking duties, she tended the family's vegetable garden, gathered wood for fires, and managed cleaning and laundry chores for her son and his family. Her constant companion was a terrier mix named Fulmine who rarely left Bianca's side and who lived up to his name by being as fast as lightning.

A constant presence at Le Convertoie, Bianca kept a watchful eye on my home when I was away, but she also kept a protective eye on me while I was there. She spoke no English, but as I grew more competent in Italian, she began to share stories about growing up in Tuscany. I was simply "la signora" or "l'americana" since "Kyle" was difficult for her to pronounce. Clearly a favorite, I would find a loaf of her coveted bread on my door wrapped in an old plastic bag, often with vine-ripened tomatoes or a head of lettuce from the garden tossed in for good measure. We fondly referred to the bread as "the Dentist's Delight" because if it wasn't eaten *subito* (immediately) on the day it was baked, the salt-less dough became as hard as a rock.

One chilly fall evening, Bianca stopped by just in time to see the kitchen filling with smoke. (I had forgotten to see if the flue was open.) After the smoke had cleared, Bianca patiently showed me how to lay the kindling and wood in a crisscross fashion, using a special inflammatory brick named *Diavolo* (Devil) just beneath the pyre. The fire roared to life under her expert guidance, this time with the flue open.

Bianca rarely asked for favors, but one morning she had a special request and wondered if I was going to Greve later. I eagerly agreed in order to have the opportunity to spend time with her. She had long ago given up driving the winding road from town to Le Convertoie, and a family member always served as her official chauffeur.

At the appointed hour, Bianca was waiting in the parking lot with two huge burlap bags filled with her freshly baked loaves. I loaded the bread into the back and indicated with a bow and a flourish that the front seat was all hers. Instead, she hopped into the back behind the driver's side with a sprightly leap that would have put an Olympic gymnast to shame. As I eased behind the wheel, my passenger gave my headrest a couple of quick slaps and announced, *"Andiamo!"* (Let's go!) I had been drafted for delivery duty, and we gamely set off on our appointed rounds with Bianca pointing out spots along the way that required my attention, most notably a dangerous curve on the road marked with numerous crosses. Our loaves duly delivered, I deposited my priceless cargo and her empty bags in the center of town.

My quest to renovate the church left Bianca, as well as most Italians I came in contact with, mystified. When I tried to explain my plans, she would shake her head and mumble something under her breath that sounded suspiciously like, "*Oh, Dio! Aiuta la pazza americana.*" ("Oh God! Help the crazy American.") She would quiz me on what the architect and construction crews were up to, asking pointed questions about the skeletons buried underneath the floor of the ancient structure. At that stage in the renovation process, we were nowhere near the point where we would be pulling up the old floor and installing a new one. "Leave them alone, signora," Bianca admonished with a wagging finger held close to my nose. A quick sign of the cross, a rushed Hail Mary, and she was off to do more chores with her trusty sidekick following closely on her heels.

Le Convertoie is a working farm, and the field below was home to several chicken coops, along with one annoyingly vocal rooster. One evening, I discovered Bianca and her son sitting side by side on the wall in front of our door. They chatted companionably while plucking feathers from two freshly slaughtered chickens from the farmyard below. When I explained that most Americans prowl the supermarket aisles, buying their chicken plucked and wrapped in plastic, they shrugged in harmony and seemed genuinely sad about the sorry state of poultry procurement in the States.

Bianca's uniform consisted of a black shift, sensible shoes, and a bandana tied jauntily around her unkempt gray hair. She carried a sturdy stick that she used to navigate the steep hills around Le Convertoie, along with a cell phone she would shake and curse when the reception failed, which was most of the time. If asked to pose for a photo by visitors, Bianca would protest loudly and once again gaze toward heaven asking forgiveness. *"Sono troppo vecchia, signora,"* (I am too old)," she would proclaim, while grinning and quickly edging her way into the middle of the shot.

Bianca was diagnosed with cancer in the spring of 2006, and her health declined rapidly. She stopped working at Le Convertoie, and Chuck and I made a visit to her apartment just before heading back to Florida. Although she still displayed some of her old familiar spunk, she seemed ready to find peace and relief from the pain. She lived in a third floor walk-up with no elevator, and until a few days before her death she was still climbing the steep stairs on her own with very little assistance. Welcoming us with a hug and a sigh, she offered an espresso and then held both of our hands, squeezing them with all her might. In a particularly heartbreaking moment, Bianca produced a photo of her beloved dog, who had died just a month earlier. She cried out his name several times and wondered if Fulmine would be waiting for her in heaven. Pointing to a cemetery in the hills above town, she said she expected to be buried there soon. We said a tearful good-bye, acutely aware of the fact we would never see each other again. She passed away just a day after our departure on April 30, 2006.

Bianca was a wonderful friend and ally, and I felt strangely protected when I returned to Le Convertoie after she died. In fact, I had very few issues with the ghostly presence afterward, and I fondly pictured her threatening anyone up above—or on earth—with some serious consequences for troubling her friend, *la signora americana.*

THERE ARE NO RULES!

If you are renovating a house in Italy, you often need to be on site, and I traveled back and forth between our two countries on a regular basis. Security and terrorist threats, mechanical and weather delays, oversized seatmates, and overworked flight attendants all added to the festive nature of the journey. In addition, frequent *scioperi* or strikes by airline, railway, train, or bus employees are a fact of life. Italians are used to these disruptions and will quickly break rank as chaos reigns.

In an episode of the NBC TV classic *30 Rock,* Alec Baldwin commented to Tina Fey, "I know this sounds ugly, but in Manhattan real estate, there are no rules. It's like check-in at an Italian airport."[12]

Author Beppe Severgnini, who wrote *La Bella Figura: A Field Guide to the Italian Mind,*[13] explains, "Italy has too much style to be hell but is too disorderly to be heaven." If you understand these basic tenets, traveling will go a lot more smoothly for you there. After living there for eleven years, I felt that I was often at cross-purposes with my adopted land, but I'd learned it was possible to be critical and protective of Italian culture at the same time.

To explain the Italian mindset further, Chuck and I, along with Lou and Maurizio, bought tickets to see American singer Sheryl Crow live in Lucca. Lucca is a charming, walled city halfway between Florence and Pisa, with a Renaissance-era pedestrian area filled with artisanal shops and restaurants. Although firmly on the tourist radar, it doesn't have the large number of day-trippers that many other famous Tuscan towns face during the summer months. In July, the city hosts an extraordinary lineup of musical talent in the outdoor arena of Piazza Napoleone in the center of town. Sting and Santana, John Legend and Los Lobos, Il Volo and Elton John—all have been featured artists in the cozy concert venue, whose motto is, "Huge Names in a Picturesque Setting!"

The weather was perfect, with starry skies and a light breeze, as we arrived for the nine o'clock evening concert. Tickets in hand, we were waved through the entrance and made our way to our assigned seats, which were already occupied. We shrugged, took someone else's seats a few rows back, and enjoyed the show. The extra money for the center row seats, the early arrival—*non ha importanza*. Italians sit where they want, when they want, and you should do the same.

Attending Siena's Palio is one of the best ways to learn more about Italian culture. Dario Castagno's greatest passion is the horse race held twice each summer in July and August in the central plaza in Siena, Piazza del Campo, called the Palio. He can obtain tickets and serve as a guide for this extraordinary event and proudly belongs to his adopted *contrada*,

Bruco, or Caterpillar neighborhood. There are seventeen con-trade in Siena, and each has a fanatical following of locals who grew up in their associated neighborhood. It's unlikely for outsiders to become members, although some succeed, including Dario and his frequent coauthor from Chicago, Robert Rodi. (Rodi wrote a humorous memoir about his effort to become one of the Caterpillars in *Seven Seasons in Siena, My Quixotic Quest for Acceptance Among Italy's Proudest People*.[14])

The enthusiasm and loyalty for the Sienese contrade and all the organized eating and drinking involved are unique to the Palio festivities. A neighborhood banquet precedes each race, and the city becomes an impromptu open-air restaurant with tables that stretch for miles on end down the ancient squares and streets. Group songs and countless toasting in honor of the jockey continue well into the night.

Only one horse can win, and sometimes the winner is riderless. Rules permit complex *partiti* (deals) among the contrade, money changes hands; what non-Sienese would judge as bribery, locals simply call strategy. Jockeys, making things even more complicated, are liable to make last-minute deals on the starting line, causing the action to halt for hours on end.

In August 2007, we joined Dario to watch the famous race from an advantaged viewpoint. Bleachers encircling the historic Piazza del Campo are packed with thousands of excited fans and tourists, some of whom stand for hours in the middle of the course/piazza. The race is preceded by a lengthy pageant called the *Corteo Storico*, comprised of handsome men in tights and traditional medieval costumes, proudly carrying their colorful banners.

After several false starts and stops, the breathtaking three-lap race erupted. Fans cheered as the jockeys slapped their horses with leather whips for the ninety-second race, and on that hot, steamy day in August, the *Leocorno (Unicorn)* triumphed. All hell broke loose as *contradaioli* poured out of the stands and central piazza to congratulate the horse and jockey. Several people ran onto the course before the race was finished, dodging the remaining horses and creating a chaotic scene.

The winning jockey was jubilantly carried on the crowd's shoulders around the course, his contrada ecstatic. I wouldn't have been surprised if the horse had been carried away on their shoulders, too. Grown men burst into tears of joy or became inconsolable at the loss, and we witnessed firsthand the thrill of victory and the agony of defeat from our snug bleacher seats.

In a perfect world, it takes twenty hours door-to-door to travel to Italy from Florida. It is always with a sense of dread that I board Italy's national airline, Alitalia. Alitalia as an acronym apparently stands for, "Always Late in Takeoffs, Always Late in Arrivals." I'm assuming "We Fly Like We Drive!" was not feasible from a marketing standpoint. Italians are known for their reckless motoring habits, which is to be expected from the country that invented the Ferrari, the Lamborghini, and the Maserati. You are required to drive on the highway at supersonic speeds just to stay alive. Weaving in and out of traffic, allowing your vehicle to wander into the adjoining lanes while texting, passing on curves on narrow village streets—*tutto regolare*. Italian pilots apply those same reckless habits in the flight deck, and you can expect Alitalia to lose your luggage and experience unexplained delays with surly, albeit impeccably turned out, flight attendants.

My worst trip on Alitalia occurred soon after 9/11. Tensions were high, and there were plenty of empty seats on the Milan to Florence flight as travelers put off all but essential travel. Visibility was poor with a steady downpour as we taxied down the runway. Bumping up to cruising altitude for the brief thirty-five-minute flight, the plane hit a pocket of turbulence that sent it lurching through the clouds. The flight attendants battened down the hatches as the passengers gripped their armrests or reached for the airsickness bags. Suddenly, an ear-splitting crash reverberated through the cabin. There were several gasps and then silence as everyone mentally ran through the possible scenarios. After watching the horrific scenes from New York, Pennsylvania, and Washington, DC, unfold just days earlier, there wasn't a single person on the plane who didn't think a bomb had exploded onboard.

As the entire cabin watched in amazement, both flight attendants sprinted from the back of the plane to the front, pulling the shabby curtain dividing the main cabin from the cockpit decisively behind them. There wasn't a single word of explanation or reassurance from the flight deck. After what seemed like an eternity, a woman's voice with a distinctly New York accent from a few rows ahead of me called out calmly, "That was not a bomb. A bolt of lightning hit the plane. There is no serious damage to the wing and no fire, but judging from the speed of our flight attendants' exit, it's possible that they took a direct hit up their asses." Laughter and applause erupted throughout the cabin, and we soon landed safely in Florence, with the entire Alitalia cabin crew leading the charge off the plane.

On another Milan to Florence trip on Alitalia in February, a thunderstorm diverted us from Florence to Verona.

As we descended through the clouds, numerous assurances were given that transportation would be arranged for all passengers to get to Florence by bus. When asked how long the bus ride would be, a sincere looking attendant replied, "Only an hour or so." A few passengers laughed out loud at this remarkable statement since, in a perfect world, this trip would easily take hours, and it would be several more before the buses showed up. But, like lambs to the slaughter, the majority of passengers duly collected their luggage and trudged out of the terminal toward the "soon to arrive" autobus. The rest of us sprinted toward the Hertz counter or grabbed a taxi for the train station.

I was once caught "hitchhiking" in Milan when all flights had been grounded due to bad weather. There was mass chaos at the airport, but I heard a muffled announcement over the PA system requesting that all passengers on BA flight 2210 should immediately board the bus for Florence. Although I had arrived on an Alitalia flight, I quickly boarded the bus, which was empty with the exception of a couple of Brits who spoke Italian, along with the flight crew. One of the flight attendants asked what seat I had been in, and I sheepishly confessed I had not been on their flight but needed to get to Florence as soon as possible. Everyone shrugged their shoulders, murmured "Ah, beh," and went back to checking their cell phones. The majority of the BA flight's passengers were left to fend for themselves at the Milan airport.

On a flight from Rome to Florence, I was seated in the first row's window seat with a bird's eye view of a unique event. One of the pilots casually left the plane with what appeared to be a large roll of tape in his hand. He reappeared at the right-hand side of the plane and pulled a small ladder up to the cockpit area. Meticulously measuring out several pieces of masking tape, he began to apply them to the side of the plane to an area about the size of a FedEx overnight package. I was startled at the rudimentary nature of the repairs but decided that if the pilot reboarded the plane, I would stay on board, too. There had to be some basic sense of self-preservation at work here.

Apparently, his handiwork exceeded his high standards for exterior airline repair, and he strolled back to the cockpit. His mission had caught the attention of several other passengers, and a heated battle to disembark ensued, with airport security arriving to quell the disturbance. Those of us who stayed onboard arrived safely.

Renting a car in Italy can be summed up by an experience Chuck had at the Hertz counter in Milan. Arriving early one morning, he was surprised by the cheerful agent's offer to personally show him to his vehicle, but dutifully followed her to the parking area. She hopped into the car, honked the horn three times and explained, "That is the horn. That is all you need to know."

Florence's airport is always under construction, and the rental car agencies are constantly being relocated. Hertz, Avis, and the ever-popular Europcar rotate their offices between a trailer, unmarked huts, and a van used by employees for chain smoking, coffee breaks, and office flirtations. Hertz "upgraded" their rental trailer by making it impossible to speak with an agent unless you ducked down and yelled through a tiny kiosk window. Rental vehicles are parked a long way from the agency "offices," and there are no lane or space numbers. Check the key number, match it to the license number, or simply walk back and forth along the aisles and continue pressing the key until one of the cars beeps at you. They now have a train that goes directly from the airport to the main train station at Santa Maria Novella. Take that and save yourself a lot of hassles.

Fueling up is a challenge since Italian pumps don't accept foreign credit cards. Gas stations can close for lunch, holidays, on Sunday afternoons, or simply because no one feels like working. Italian road signs can be misleading, as there may be several choices leading in different directions, but all supposedly going to the same place. No one slows or stops for yellow lights, and stop signs are just a suggestion. All hell breaks loose on the roundabouts, and unless you make eye contact with the driver who is supposed to yield, don't even think about pulling out. "White roads," although beloved by Italians as shortcuts, are often treacherously winding gravel roads that can take the unsuspecting traveler miles out of their way. Pull out your cell phone—there will be no service—and cry out of sheer frustration, but at least the scenery is gorgeous.

L'ULTIMA ANTICA POSTA

The Italians have many frequently quoted adages, such as *Natale con i tuoi, Pasqua con chi vuoi,* or "Christmas with your family, Easter with whomever you want." In architecture, a time-honored saying is, *Per un edificio vecchio, c'è bisogno di oggetti antichi:* "For an old building, you require antiques." Okay, I took a little artistic license with this second one, but it goes without saying that you should not go to IKEA to furnish a centuries-old structure.

If it wasn't already abundantly clear, let me admit that shopping in Italy is one of my greatest pleasures. Chuck often tells friends, "I'm in procurement, and she's in distribution." I was on a mission to find just the right pieces for our home. Susan often accompanied me, and one of our regular destinations was Arezzo for the monthly antiques market. We found a weathered yellow iron garden base that, with a glass top added, became a coffee table, while a painted blue buffet served admirably in the dining room. The upholstered pieces and curtains for the dining room were ordered in the States, purely from the standpoint of ease of measuring, designing, and selecting materials in English. Susan found all the dining and side chairs in Hickory, North Carolina, and then had an upholsterer in Florida make the custom pieces, shipping everything over to Italy in one container. The custom sectional sleep sofa, upholstered in a textured blue tweed fabric, anchored the room, while an old wooden desk, a consignment store find, was paired with an antique throne chair in a corner.

An eighteenth-century wooden angel without a face, a spectacular object in robin's egg blue and gold, became a wall hanging in the *sacrestia*. After purchasing her in Arezzo at a small antiques store, we realized we would have a hard time retrieving her, even if we were on foot in broad daylight. Setting a course through the middle of town during rush hour in our rented station wagon, we were hampered by one-way streets and dead ends. We finally turned onto the shop's "mostly for pedestrians" location at closing time. In my haste, I sideswiped a wall and took out the passenger side mirror, coming to a screeching halt in front of the store moments before it closed. Susan and I soon emerged from the shop, struggling to haul the angel the few feet to the car. The angel was a lot heavier than she looked, and we could not fit her into the vehicle. Pushing, cussing in two languages, and shoving with all our might, we finally found a spot for the celestial T-shaped pediment next to the gear shift. Susan spent the journey back to Greve wedged against the car door, nose-to-nose with a faceless form with an enormous wingspan. A skilled craftsman from Panzano gave her a new countenance, and from then on she followed guests as they walked through the room with a steady, slightly cross-eyed gaze.

Part of the sacrestia space was turned into a bathroom, adding a much-needed second shower, toilet, and a pedestal sink. A ceramic plaque "in the style of Della Robbia" of the Virgin and Child was hung above the sink. It was an effort to rein in the "leap of faith" theme, but we approached it with a sense of reverence, not wanting it to look too much like . . . well, a church.

"It's all about the journey, not the destination," but some of my purchases might not agree. In London, at the prestigious annual Olympia Art and Antiques Fair, I scored one of my biggest finds. The areas above the two altars in the church's living area were problematic since we didn't want to overdo it.

A Dutch vendor at the fair proudly displayed a carved wooden religious figure he described as a seventeenth-century bishop. Its origins were uncertain, although the dealer assigned the carving to Germany in the 1600s. The statue's back was so charred and disfigured by a fire that had occurred hundreds of years earlier that the elegant, curved lines of his robe had completely disappeared. The front of the statue was untouched and perched on a neatly squared wooden pedestal. The Bishop met my gaze with a solemn, stately grace. I knew he was perfect, but I was worried about shipping the sixty-pound statue from London to Florence.

When I mentioned my problem to one of the salespeople, Anna, she immediately replied that she loved Italy and would bring the statue down herself. The unlikely traveling duo scored two seats on Ryanair from Amsterdam into Pisa the following week. The plane was delayed for hours because of a blinding rainstorm, but Anna finally appeared in the baggage claim area with her precious cargo. The Bishop looked as if he had enjoyed the ride, the same benevolent smile greeting me from his new location inside a cavernous black tennis racquet bag. Anna headed off on the train to Florence, where I had fittingly booked her overnight accommodations at a convent.

The wall above the second altar posed a further challenge. There was no niche as there was on the Bishop's side of the room, simply a large blank space. One evening, purely by chance, I drove past an antiques store in the industrial town of Figline Valdarno, just outside of Florence. Prominently displayed in the front window of the shop was a large painting of a priest lovingly presenting baby Jesus to a group of devoted admirers at the temple. The priest's brilliant gold vestments shone in the single light of the shop's window, while a woman kneeling in prayer at his feet wore a lapis-blue robe and scarf. The oil painting was so beautiful that I stood staring at it well after night fell. I knew it would be perfect in the space and returned the next day to take photos and measurements. Luckily for me, the shopkeeper's niece from the States was visiting, and she translated the history of the painting. It had come from a small church near San Casciano, and the antiques dealer was very familiar with Le Convertoie and the renovation project. He agreed to a try-out in the space, bringing the painting in the back of his van the next day. When it was placed over the altar, it took my breath away and was clearly meant to hang there. Sold to the pazza americana for a small fortune!

The priest, baby Jesus, and his followers suffered a terrible indignity when left hanging in the humid church over the summer months. We considered installing dehumidifiers, but there was nowhere to drain the water and no one available to empty the pans on a daily basis. When I returned in September after a long, hot summer, the entire canvas was covered in a thick, fluffy, grayish mold. The humidity in the closed church, coupled with the ancient cloth backing on the painting, had created the perfect breeding ground for some kind of fuzzy fungus. In a complete state of jetlagged panic, I pulled it down from its spot above the altar and cleaned it with a soft cloth and some Lysol. It then dried in the open air propped unceremoniously on chairs in the backyard. I could have easily ruined it, but my crude method worked, and the painting dried out with very little damage.

Figline turned out to be an unlikely goldmine as far as furniture shopping was concerned. There is not much of interest in the town unless you include the massive COOP grocery store frequented by budget-minded tourists vacationing in an RV camp nearby. Figline's biggest claim to fame is its part-time resident, rock icon Sting, who owns a spectacular sixteenth-century villa nearby called Il Palagio. Sting and his wife, Trudie Styler, purchased the property in the late 1990s and restored the villa, offering organic wine, olive oil, and honey grown on the estate.

I stumbled on a warehouse with room after room of treasures in Figline. The only problem with shopping there was the owner, a quirky little man with tastes that fell well outside of the world of interior design. He unabashedly displayed a creepy collection of pornographic magazines throughout the shop. No matter where you looked, pictures of well-endowed models could be found posing from the seat of a beautifully upholstered settee, in the drawers of an eighteenth-century armoire, or on the shelf of a French curio cabinet. There were years of back issues of the Italian edition of *Playboy* piled in neat stacks in the ladies' room. I am ashamed to say that his prices were so reasonable that I overlooked his questionable lifestyle pursuits and bought quite a few pieces of furniture from him, including a beautiful farmhouse-style dining room table. When it was delivered, I realized why it was such a deal. The table legs were too high, making anyone sitting at the table feel like Lily Tomlin's character Edith Ann. My brother-in-law had to saw off a considerable amount of wood on the legs to make it usable.

Italy is a shopaholic's dream when searching for ceramics, and the Umbrian region's tiny town of Deruta is famous for its exquisite tableware, mosaics, and porcelain. Two sorority sisters of mine, Janice and Sharon, made the two-hour drive with me from Greve one fine spring morning, stopping to watch a charming artisan throw pottery in his downstairs workshop. To demonstrate his craft in a more personal way, the potter gently drew Janice to his wheel, dramatically recreating the scene from the 1990 film *Ghost*.[15] It was as if Patrick Swayze were there with Demi Moore, his spirit full of love and longing, still palpable months after his death. Janice played Demi's part admirably, swooning and swaying as they formed their clay masterpiece together. Naturally, we all appreciated the marketing effort and purchased several items.

In the hilltop town of Castellina in Chianti, La Bottega featured an eclectic array of antiques, paintings, Venetian glassware, and wall hangings. Owner Mario Cappelletti can trace his family tree back to Verona's star-crossed lover, Juliet, and he's a devoted collector of Russian icons. The exquisitely painted wooden panels, dating from the fifteenth and sixteenth century, were tucked away at the back of the shop, and the icons were believed to heal and work miracles if kissed, symbolizing medieval faith in an extraordinarily simple, stunning style. The icon I bought from Mario had been fashioned out of dark, hand-painted wood with four different versions of the Virgin Mary circling a vision of Jesus on the cross. It sat proudly at the entrance to the nave on an old wooden trunk, also a purchase from Mario.

PASSING THE TORCH FROM
MARINELLA TO LORI

We relied on Marinella Coppi for so many things during our years at Le Convertoie. She was principally a real estate agent, no small feat in a culture where women are expected to fulfill the traditional role of marrying, cooking for the family, and raising children. Mari courageously opened her own real estate office in Greve and agreed to manage things at Le Convertoie while we were away. She had grown up in Greve and helped Vidotto negotiate the ins and outs at the Comune di Greve, shared neighborhood gossip with me, and always listened to my rants and raves with an open mind and a quiet sense of amusement.

We became such good friends that I had the pleasure of being invited to her thirtieth birthday party, held at a popular nightclub in Florence. Betsy was in town, and we knew it would be dangerous to drive back to Greve after the party, so we stayed at the Plaza Lucchese, a lovely, family-owned hotel on the Arno.

Betsy and I ate dinner at the Lucchese, assuming it would be a drinks and hors d'oeuvre party. Strolling into the private dining area around nine o'clock, we were greeted by a round of applause. Not only were we the only Americans, but we were fashionably late, quite a coup on both counts.

As the evening wore on, the Italian men in the group became jolly and boisterous. The butcher, the baker, a grocer, and a pizza maker—all from Greve—grabbed lit candlesticks and began singing and dancing their way through the crowded bar area. The party spilled out onto the adjacent terrace, and I happily joined the conga line, completely unaware that Betsy was frozen in fear in a far corner of the dining room. She had noticed what I had not—the drunken guests, swaying to and fro, were dangerously close to setting the wooden building on fire, along with the packed disco hall below.

We left around two in the morning and couldn't find a cab, so we had to walk several miles back to the hotel. Betsy claims she still has nightmares about Marinella's birthday bash.

Marinella was contacted by HGTV's *House Hunters International*,[16] promising to showcase her current listings and guaranteeing to attract more clients. The filming process was lengthy, involving a full week's commitment for the shoot. Mari was asked to come up with an attractive couple—ostensibly looking at three different properties in the Greve area—destined to celebrate their own epiphany at the end of the thirty-minute show.

Mari had never heard of *House Hunters International* and asked whether it was worth the time to participate. I admitted finding the patented process of the search, followed by the couples' discussion of their dilemma of which house to choose over drinks, entertaining. The show's staff didn't care who starred in the episode, and it was worth a shot to boost real estate sales, so Marinella asked a couple from Greve—an American woman and her Dutch husband—to appear with her.

We owned the apartment and church at that point, but we were only starting on permitting. The renovation was still in the planning stage, and the church was uninhabitable—not exactly ready for its close-up. The couple had already purchased one of the homes they were touring in the show, but they dutifully looked at three different properties, including ours, which wasn't for sale, oohing and ahhing and discussing the pros and cons ad nauseum. Marinella never got any business as a result of the show, and the starring couple, clearly star-crossed, separated soon afterwards.

Marinella's business was a full-time job, and she was not prepared to be a 24/7 property manager for us. I have an email from her dated April 15, 2005, giving an indication of the problems she was constantly dealing with at Le Convertoie. She had struggled with the Italian-to-English translation, which made the message even more charming. "Dear Guests, We are sorry for the washing machine that will be repair until Wednesday 20 aprile. In the meant time if you need to use it, please, call Mrs. Cristina the Lady who think to clean the house and she will be happy to help you. Please, I will be very glad to know when the repairman could came to the house without make noise to you." When some acquaintances from Florida visiting Le Convertoie asked Mari to find a car repair shop to fix a dent they had put in their rental vehicle, she was too sweet to say no. It was clearly time to hire someone else.

I researched Florentine companies that specialized in the rental market and discovered a firm called Pitcher & Flaccomio, based in an ancient palazzo near the Arno. I felt an immediate rapport with Corso Flaccomio, co-owner of the company and a childhood friend of Gabriele Corso of the Food TV Network's hit show *Extra Virgin.* Corso listened patiently as I outlined my requirements for managing our property and said he had the perfect person for us, California native Lori Hetherington. Lori had moved to Florence years earlier, married an Italian, and worked for Pitcher & Flaccomio handling rental properties for many of the company's English-speaking clientele. Blond and petite, Lori is organized, fluent in Italian, and has a fair but decisive way of dealing with problems. Her email updates on Le Convertoie were always concise and informative, and she managed the property with diplomacy and efficiency. I think Marinella was relieved to have the burden of Le Convertoie behind her.

LA FESTA

After the three-year-long renovation of the church was completed, it was time to celebrate and thank everyone with a *festa* or party for friends and family, both Italian and American. Neighbors who had to put up with the construction, people who had to listen to me complain endlessly about the construction, the banker who allowed me to pay for the construction, and Vidotto and the construction crew—all were welcome. A date was set for the first weekend in November 2008, and I set up a website, announcing the party as "A Gathering of Saints and Sinners." Sue and I met with a popular Florentine catering firm, Convivium, finally deciding on a menu that included truffled French fries and fried sage in brown paper, grilled meats, chicken, and vegetables, and tiramisu for dessert—all prepared on site. Tignanello, one of Italy's best super Tuscan reds, would be served. We invited over fifty guests from the States—erroneously thinking that most of them would decline—but almost every invitee RSVP'd

"Yes." Our son, Josh, and daughter-in-law, Liz, arrived and announced they were expecting a baby, our first grandchild, so the weekend was kicked off with a wonderful surprise and even more reason to celebrate.

I planned the festa from the standpoint of staging a destination weekend, setting up a series of events that I hoped everyone would enjoy. On Thursday night, a few early arrivals had a casual dinner at our house catered by the butcher of Panzano's sister-in-law. On Friday, we toured the nearby vineyard at Castello di Verrazzano, rumored to be the spot where Da Vinci painted the *Mona Lisa*, followed by lunch and a lecture on Tuscan history by Dario Castagno. After lunch, as if on cue, a rainbow appeared off the terrace, providing a spectacular photo op.

That evening, Sue organized two vans that ferried the American guests to a dinner at La Cantinetta di Rignana, a cozy restaurant in the countryside twenty minutes outside of Greve. To our amazement, a wild boar appeared on the road, seemingly wishing us a good evening. Course after course arrived and was served family style, in large ceramic dishes passed along the tables, with copious amounts of wine accompanying the meal. Toward the end of the evening, Chuck went to the office to pay our bill, which was considerable. His Mastercard was denied, then his Visa, and when the American Express card didn't go through, Chuck, sweating profusely, came out and whispered that my presence was urgently needed in the office. The restaurant owner looked skeptical after three card denials in a row and I briefly imagined passing a hat asking for donations, but my Italian Visa went through and everyone happily poured back into the vans unaware of the emergency.

Some of our rowdier friends rented a cluster of hotel rooms at the Albergo del Chianti on the piazza in Greve. The Saturday market and proximity to Le Convertoie made it a perfect place to stay, although the continuous party atmosphere apparently caused the innkeeper, Francesco, to say, "*Basta!*" After an initial request to wrap it up at the Albergo's bar went unheeded, Francesco pulled up a chair and pretended to hang himself with a large rope. On Sunday at checkout, when the group merrily promised to return soon, Francesco pulled a (hopefully unloaded) shotgun out from behind the check-in desk and threatened to shoot himself. They assumed he was just being dramatic.

The weekend wouldn't have been complete without an appearance by our ghost. On the morning of the party, I got an early wake-up call from our housekeeper. She explained she had been called three times during the night from the landline phone of the "big villa," which we had rented for overflow guests. The property had been on the market for many years, although beautifully situated with a pool and spectacular views of the countryside, and our housekeeper was the caretaker for that house as well.

The first call came to our housekeeper's cell phone at one in the morning, and a female voice in English simply said, "Help me!" There is very little crime in Greve, and our daughter, Tracy, and two friends had the only extra key. Our housekeeper tried to return the call but got a busy signal, so she put the call down to a miscommunication. The second call came at two, the same message in a plaintive, pleading voice in English. At this point, our housekeeper became truly alarmed and tried repeatedly to call me, but we had no cell phone service in the apartment. (To be honest, we had gotten home at midnight and were out cold.) The third call, the most urgent but with the same message, came at three o'clock. Our housekeeper and her husband then drove to Le Convertoie and knocked on our door. We didn't hear them, so they found their way in the pitch dark to the villa where they knocked again and again without any success there either.

The couple reluctantly went home and then returned at eight o'clock. As she recounted the trio of petrifying phone calls, I started to panic. She and I ran from the apartment to the villa and began pounding on the door. There was no answer. We found a spare key at a remote location near the pool and gained entry to the home, finding all three occupants fast asleep and unharmed. The only thing out of the ordinary was the 1950s-style telephone in the entryway, off the hook and dangling precariously from the console.

Sue and Fabio stayed at the same villa the night of the party and woke the next morning to find the bathroom filled with dead flies. They were everywhere, stuck to the white ceiling, the white tiled walls, and the ornate Venetian mirror. There were no open windows, providing no obvious reason for such a monumental mass insetti suicide, but Sue and I had fun trading a few *Lord of the Flies* references. Fabio, who has an intense dislike of spiders and other insects, had come prepared with a can of Raid and handily finished off the few remaining survivors. There weren't many questions about why the villa hadn't sold after that weekend.

During the day on Saturday, a cooking class with two local chefs demonstrated the art of making fresh pasta for a few of our guests. Others spent the day in Florence and Siena or strolling through the farmer's market in Greve. In the late afternoon, the caterers arrived, buffets were set up, candles were lit, and the church's renovation was ready for its close-up.

At that point, I resembled Norma Desmond in *Sunset Boulevard* and was acting a little off-kilter. But as the guests arrived, everything fell into place, and we toasted the gorgeous church with bubbling glasses of Prosecco. The early November evening air was clear and cool, and our guests settled in, mingled, and enjoyed the evening. I'm assuming most of them were relieved not to have to listen to me talk about the construction woes anymore. Drinks and hors d'oeuvres were set up in the cantina, and the party spilled out into the backyard, where *bistecca alla fiorentina* and herb-infused, roasted chicken sizzled on the grills above the graves. It was a party to remember because of the people who were there, and our beautiful Le Convertoie more than rose to the occasion.

The party was over, and after a hectic Sunday bidding fond farewells and ferrying family and friends to the airport, the chapel was ready for Kim Sargent's photo shoot. Kim and Joan had returned just to shoot Le Convertoie in its finest hour, with the hope that *Architectural Digest*[17] would be interested in featuring the property in a "Before and After" issue. I was out of steam by then and panicked when Kim suggested a photo with Susan, Vidotto, and me in front of the *Presentation of Jesus at the Temple* painting in the church's nave. I am surely the only person in *AD*'s venerated history wearing a wrinkled Eileen Fisher cardigan set I fished out of the bottom of the laundry basket for the owner/architect/designer shot.

We all kept our fingers crossed as Kim submitted the photos to *Architectural Digest*'s editor Paige Rense Noland for her approval. Several months went by, but finally the editors notified Susan that the story would be featured in the March 2010 issue. Susan, Vidotto, and I were asked to fill out detailed questionnaires about the project. The author, John Loring, was head designer for the jewelry giant Tiffany & Co. in New York and has written several books about the company. He wrote the eight-page feature, entitled "Classical Epiphany," based solely on the photos and did an excellent job of conveying how the restoration evolved. The issue featured actress Jennifer Aniston on the cover in her new home in Beverly Hills, so we were in good company.

THE FINAL *ATTO*

I'm not sure of the exact moment when it changed from the apple of my eye to a problem child, but in 2010 after the article appeared, we decided to put Le Convertoie on the market. The party was over, the mission accomplished, and it became increasingly harder to spend time in Italy. Our beautiful first granddaughter, Peyton Laurel, was born, and life changes dramatically (for the better) after grandchildren arrive on the scene. My parents' health declined, and they had several emergencies requiring us to spend long stretches of time in Florida. The day-to-day upkeep of Le Convertoie became more about taking care of what we had refurbished for visitors than using our home ourselves.

As is the usual custom in Italy, I listed Le Convertoie with multiple resources. Marinella was an obvious choice, but we also gave Pitcher & Flaccomio the listing, along with a prestigious British firm, Knight Frank, which had a branch office in nearby Radda-in-Chianti. As the months wore on without a solid offer, I began to worry if we would ever be able to sell it, but it was Marinella who brought in the buyer, and if all went well, she would sell the property twice.

The light at the end of the tunnel was a red-headed British expat named Kate, who had lived in Florence for several years, a professor who spoke fluent Italian and was enthralled with Le Convertoie from the first time she visited. Kate was an ideal purchaser since she had cash and was ready to close immediately, but this was Italy and a historic property, so that wasn't realistic. She was as enthusiastic about Le Convertoie's restoration as we had been, and if you have to sell a place that you have put your heart and soul into, it's a consolation to sell to someone who truly cares.

One of my least attractive personality traits is that when I'm done, I'm done. Maybe it's because of all the moves I've made in life, but I have a strange lack of sentimentality and can walk away from someplace, even if I've loved it and lived there a long time, without looking back. The years of struggling to restore it, the pride of accomplishment I had when the project was completed—I put all that behind me, realizing the impracticality of living there any longer. Once I decided to do it, I was so eager to sell Le Convertoie that I accepted Kate's first offer, even adding in some furnishings that I knew couldn't be moved out without a great deal of difficulty.

Kate put down the initial deposit and hired an inspector/architect. She wanted to put a pool in, but I discouraged that idea since there was the slight problem of a possible ossuary in the back yard. There would also be no water to fill the pool, but that was a minor point considering the bigger picture.

Our land included not only the parking lot, but also a small plot of land below Le Convertoie that abutted the neighbor's chicken coop and vegetable garden. When Kate petitioned the Comune di Greve for permission to put in a swimming pool in that area, the petition was rejected, but they encouraged installation of a *vasca di irrigazione*, an agricultural drainage ditch for the poultry population. Strangely enough, she never followed through on that.

We also owned a small, wooded area off the parking lot that Kate was concerned about. "Whose responsibility is it to keep that area clean?" she asked sincerely. Considering the fact that no one but the neighbor's dogs set foot in the space, her concern seemed unwarranted, but we admired her attention to detail.

Kate's architect decided there was not enough fresh air coming into the chapel. The original double doors of the church opened, and we had two sets of windows in the sacristy that allowed a nice airflow from front to back. A self-admitted alarmist, he demanded that we drill a hole in the wall of the chapel to fix the problem. We rejected that suggestion outright. In the kitchen, he worried about a potential gas leak. Kate would pay for an electric stovetop if we would pay for installation, and we agreed just to keep the process moving.

Throughout the months-long purchase process, Sue, Marinella, and Lori constantly fielded document demands, appeased Kate's inspector, and answered legitimate concerns from the neighbors about the new owner. Marinella would receive a commission serving as the representative for both the buyer and the seller, and I paid Lori for her countless hours behind the scenes. But the sale of Le Convertoie, just like its purchase, had become a full-time job for Sue and Fabio, in addition to Sue's full-time post at FSU. I kept an email from Sue saying, "Marinella and I have remarked about your good spirits concerning all of this . . . is it just a front?" It was hard for me to complain when they were doing all the heavy lifting, and I am eternally grateful for their help.

With only a couple of days until the closing, a major curveball arrived by way of our Italian notaio. He had drawn up the original purchase documents and, apparently, in disbelief that I was buying Le Convertoie on my own, he had added Chuck's name to one of the documents. In order to buy or sell a house in Italy, you need to have a *codice fiscale,* which is similar to an American social security number, and I had applied for one at the beginning of the purchase process years earlier. Thanks to the notaio's error, Chuck now needed one, and we had no time to get it.

Serving as translator, Marinella accompanied us to the Agenzia della Entrate (tax office) in Florence and presented Chuck's application to the no-nonsense bureaucrat behind the desk. She consulted her computer, beginning a lengthy dissertation to Marinella that was difficult for me to follow, although it was hard to miss Mari's eyes widening in terror. I had understood *"andare a Roma"* and *"possono fare la richiesta li."* "They will need to go to Rome. That's the only place he can make this application."

Incredibly, there was another Charles Edward Ball with the same birthdate who already had a codice fiscale number, and this would take at least a week to ten days once we applied in person in Rome. Mari and I exchanged a look of disbelief at this bit of information, since nothing takes a week to ten days to accomplish in Italy.

Charles Ball is not exactly a common Italian name, but Chuck is in private equity, and his firm has owned several international companies over the years. The only explanation for this fluke was that when his company had bought a coffee company in Milan years earlier, with Chuck serving on the board, they applied for a codice fiscale without his knowledge.

I implored *la signora burocrata* for help in my rudimentary Italian, explaining that this was a simple misunderstanding. The woman frowned, looked up from her desk over her wire-rimmed glasses, and seemed ready to send us on the first train south. For some unknown reason, though, she suddenly smiled and printed the coveted card for Chuck, saving us a trip to Rome and a postponement of the closing. There is usually a way to get around rules that don't suit you in Italy, but sometimes you just get lucky.

The next blow came when Vidotto received a request from the Belle Arti for a final inspection of Le Convertoie after the renovation. It had been a couple of years since the construction was finished, and Vidotto had filed all the necessary papers, inviting the officials to visit on several occasions. Their approval was crucial, but their call came at an inopportune time, on the day before the closing. I referred to this problem as "stump the notaio" because he had never heard of a situation like this before.

The Belle Arti wasn't prepared to visit immediately, so we had to close with the stipulation that the property would be in Kate's name, with some of the proceeds remaining in escrow until the Belle Arti had approved the renovations. To begin the sale process again or, even worse, to have to redo any aspect of the renovation that wasn't approved was unthinkable. We hoped for the best but braced for a complete debacle. I drank a lot of wine, visited our personal confessional, and offered a flurry of Hail Mary's before their visit. This approach clearly worked, since on the day of the inspection, Vidotto had an amicable meeting, and everything was approved for Kate to be the proud new owner of Le Convertoie, including the previously unapproved recessed lights.

The sale was completed in December 2012, but there then followed a three-month waiting period to receive the funds while the Catholic Diocese considered whether they wanted to buy the church back. "Just a formality," our notaio cheerfully noted, and he was right. Another requirement was a document from the Comune di Greve that all the renovation work was properly permitted. This had to be signed by the Mayor of Greve, and Marinella spent weeks trying to get his signature. She and I laughed hysterically at the closing when that document was produced, remembering my suggestion that I should just sign it myself and save her a lot of time and effort.

Winter can be cold and rainy in Italy, and that December was no exception. Lori hired a moving company to pack up the furniture and artwork. I had tried to sell some of the items in Italy, but to no avail unless I wanted to give them away. Most of it was going to Atlanta to a home we had rented there to be closer to our new granddaughter (and another to follow in a couple of years, Lillian Elizabeth). A few items stayed because of my agreement with Kate, including a stone trough from the kitchen and a set of faded green doors that were original to the church. The movers arrived in force, and it was unsettling to watch as they crated all the beautiful items I had spent so much time collecting over the years. I needed to remind myself over and over again that there were no regrets.

Betsy and KK, my Italophile friend who had spent more time over the years at Le Convertoie than we did, came to help with the move. This was an incredibly generous act that was above and beyond, especially in December. The weather was miserable, blowing sheets of rain and wind during the three-day process. The steep entrance to Le Convertoie turned into a river of mud, making it slippery and unsafe as we trooped back and forth to the parking lot. Each evening, exhausted, we returned to a hotel on the piazza in Greve and reminisced about our times together at Le Convertoie. We were all shaken by the realization that none of us would be coming back, and Betsy presented us with T-shirts inscribed *L'Ultimo Bicchiere* (The Last Glass) with a glass of red wine pictured underneath.

It was a soggy, bittersweet farewell as we watched the moving vans drive away. Our neighbors, huddling under umbrellas, waved as we pulled out of the parking lot for the final time. We spent that night in Florence, where Sue and Lou hosted a dinner for us. We laughed, cried, and toasted all the wonderful memories and adventures we had experienced in Italy together. The realization that I wouldn't be part of my friends' lives on a regular basis suddenly hit me. A wave of sadness and finality rushed over me, but it was time to go.

Betsy, KK, and I planned to fly back to the States through Munich, where the German Christmas markets were in full swing. Our flight was scheduled to leave Florence early the next day, and we couldn't wait to stroll through the wintry wonderland filled with handcrafted ornaments, wooden pyramids, and nutcrackers. But anticipation soon turned to panic when we checked in for our Alitalia flight ("Always Late in Takeoffs") at the Florence airport. The plane was delayed because of mechanical difficulties, and our frustration grew as the day wore on with no departure in sight. It was an ironic end to my eleven years in Italy, spending eleven hours at the airport trying to make an exit. We eventually arrived in Munich ("Always Late in Arrivals"), barely making it in time to drop our bags at the hotel and rush to the Christmas market for its final hour. *Buon Natale, Alitalia!*

EPILOGUE

O
ur furniture didn't go far that December. The movers
were required to submit a list of all the items being sent
to the States in case we were illegally taking Italian antiques
out of the country. The authorities carefully inspected several
items before they could be packed and shipped, including
the Bishop, the painting from Figline, an antique church
bench, two gold-framed scrolls in Latin, the wooden angel
wall hanging, and the blue-and-white buffet in the dining
room. I was most concerned about the painting, but that
turned out to be a reproduction I had overpaid thousands of
euros for. The Bishop, however, caught their attention since
they believed he had not been sculpted in Germany, but in
Italy. If Italian, he would have to remain there, and I would
receive no compensation for his loss. The research process
took several months, and all our furniture was held in a hot
warehouse in Rome until finally approved for shipment to
Atlanta. The Bishop escaped to Georgia, where he spends

his days on a mantel in our living room there, still benevolently gazing down on us, silently blessing visitors with his charred staff.

It took eighteen months to get the remaining funds out of Italy, and I returned once more for the final closing. Chuck signed a power of attorney since he could not be present, and all the documents had to be read once again. The meeting lasted so long that we couldn't complete the closing that day. (Kate had neglected to bring a cashier's check, misunderstanding the notaio's instructions.) The proceedings poured over into the next day, but the sale was finally accomplished.

I still hear occasionally from Kate, who rents Le Convertoie out frequently via VRBO.com ("Historic Chianti house and ex-church with idyllic views"). It is a beautiful place, and I would highly recommend renting from Kate. She hasn't had any problems with ghosts, smoking or otherwise, but emailed to ask who had treated the wooden beams in the sacrestia for termites. Although I knew that task was completed, I couldn't find any reference as to who had done it in my paperwork. She wrote, "I'm hearing a rather ominous soft munching noise from the beams and fear there might be a deathwatch beetle infestation." I admired the insect's appropriate name and was thrilled it wasn't my problem anymore.

"Epiphany" means to show, and I let the church show me what it wanted to be. Winston Churchill once said, "We shape our buildings and then our buildings shape us." That is certainly true when I think back on our experiences in Italy, some funny and some frightening. The discovery of an ossuary in the backyard, an invasion of mysterious insects, and a change in Italy's national currency from the lira to the euro—all required the patience of a saint, which I clearly am not.

What I hope shines through is that it was a privilege to restore such a beautiful building. The feature on Le Convertoie's renovation in *Architectural Digest* was an incredible honor—the icing on the cake—but it never entered my mind when I first set eyes upon the church to aim for that. The challenges of working within and around the system in Italy nearly defeated me, and there were many times when I wished I'd never set eyes on the place. I stuck with it because I didn't want to let anyone down—my family and friends (both in the States and in Italy) and all the skilled artisans who worked so hard to transform the little church. There was a lot at stake, including my pride. We have never returned to Le Convertoie, although we've visited Italy several times since the sale. Sometimes you can't go home again.

It was so satisfying and heartwarming to know that everyone who visited fell in love with Le Convertoie. It served as the setting for many wonderful memories that will last a lifetime, and it will always make Chuck and me recall, with a mixture of amazement and gratitude, the life-"altar"-ing opportunities that restoring our little church afforded us.

ENDNOTES

1. E. E. Cummings: *Complete Poems 1904–1962*, edited by George James Firmage ©, Liveright, 1994.
2. Frances Mayes, *Under the Tuscan Sun* (NY, NY, Broadway Brooks, 1997).
3. E. E. Cummings, *op. cit.*
4. Elizabeth Helman Minchilli, *Restoring a Home in Italy,* (NY, NY, Artisan, A Division of Workman Publishing, 2001).
5. "The Lost Leonardo da Vinci: An Art Detective's Quest to Find a Lost Leonardo Da Vinci Masterpiece," *60 Minutes,* correspondent Morley Safer, produced by David Browning, CBS News, April 20, 2008, www.cbsnews.com/news/the-lost-leonardo-da-vinci.
6. Dan Brown, *The Da Vinci Code:* A Novel (Robert Langdon), (Anchor, 2003).
7. Dario Castagno with Robert Rodi, *Too Much Tuscan Sun: Confessions of a Chianti Tour Guide* (Globe Pequot, 2004).

8. Renato Stopani, *Le Convertoie*, Ager Clantius XIV, Centro di Studi Chiantigiani "CLANTE," Marzo 2011.

9. Rachel Donadio, "When Italians Chat, Hands and Fingers do the Talking," *New York Times*, NY Edition, July 1, 2013, Section A, page 6.

10. *Under the Tuscan Sun, op. cit.*

11. Peter Mayle, *A Year in Provence*, (Knopf Doubleday Publishing Group, June 1991).

12. Tina Fey, *30 Rock*, "Liz Lemon Makes Sun Tea," Season 4, Episode 6, Broadway Video, Little Stranger, NBC Studios.

13. Beppe Severgnini, *La Bella Figura—A Field Guide to the Italian Mind* (Broadway Books, 2008).

14. Robert Rodi, *Seven Seasons in Siena: My Quixotic Quest for Acceptance Among Italy's Proudest People* (Ballantine Books, 2011).

15. *Ghost*, Paramount Pictures, Howard W. Koch Productions, July 1990.

16. *House Hunters International*, HGTV, Season 2, Episode 9, Greve-in-Chianti.

17. *Architectural Digest*, a Conde Nast Publication, March 2010, Volume 67, Number 3. "Classical Epiphany, New Life For A Once-Abandoned Medieval Property in Italy," text by John Loring/ Photography by Kim Sargent, pages 114-121.

ACKNOWLEDGMENTS

Susan Schuyler Smith, Spectrum Interior Design, Vero Beach, Florida, and Marco Vidotto, Studio Di Architettura Vidotto, Siena, Italy, for their incredible vision, talent, and dedication to the project.

Kim and Joan Sargent, Sargent Architectural Photography, West Palm Beach, Florida, for their support and spectacular "before and after" pictures.

Betsy Tilghman, Kathy Kohlhorst Corley, and Lou Lodge, for all your visits, friendship, help with the move, and for always welcoming me at "Lou's Lodge."

Marinella Coppi, Studio Immobiliare Coppi, for helping me find Le Convertoie in the first place and selling it at the last, along with your guidance in learning the ins and outs of living in Tuscany.

Dario Castagno and Lori Hetherington, for your editorial assistance and years of help and support in Italy.

Bob and Bonny Baldock, for your construction expertise and for dealing with the "Marlboro Man" without complaint.

ABOUT THE AUTHOR

photo © Theresa Reynolds Photography

A University of Florida graduate with a degree in Sociology, Kyle Tackwell Ball worked as a court reporter in Atlanta in the early '80s before moving overseas with her family, first to London and then to Brussels. When she relocated to Vero Beach, Florida, after seven years as an expatriate, she began a career in public relations as a consultant for Moulton Media Relations. She holds an APR (Accredited in Public Relations) designation from the Florida Public Relations Association and formerly served as the organization's Treasure Coast Chapter president. She was President of Kyle Ball & Associates, a PR firm specializing in real estate, interior design, and architectural media relations and marketing, before turning to full-time renovation in Italy. *Altared* is her first book.

Author website: KyleTackwellBall.com
Author email: kyleball@mac.com

SELECTED TITLES FROM SHE WRITES PRESS

She Writes Press is an independent publishing company founded to serve women writers everywhere. Visit us at www.shewritespress.com.

A September to Remember: Searching for Culinary Pleasures at the Italian Table, Book Three by Carole Bumpus. $16.95, 978-1-63152-727-2. Join Carole Bumpus and her husband in Book Three of the Savoring the Olde Ways series as they take you on their first culinary trek through Italy—Lombardy, Tuscany, Compania, Apulia, Lazio, and more—a trip of unforgettable characters, sumptuous traditional foods, and sublime beauty.

Searching for Family and Traditions at the French Table, Book Two by Carole Bumpus. $16.95, 978-1-63152-896-5. An intimate peek inside the homes and lives of the French, a collection of traditional French recipes, and a compendium of culinary cultural traditions, sprinkled with historical anecdotes and spiced with humor and deliciously candid memories, this culinary travel memoir—the second of the Savoring the Olde Ways series—reveals French families at their best and at their own dinner tables.

Searching for Family and Traditions at the French Table, Book One by Carole Bumpus. $16.95, 978-1-63152-896-5. Part culinary memoir and part travelogue, this compilation of intimate interviews, conversations, stories, and traditional family recipes (cuisine pauvre) in the kitchens of French families, gathered by Carole Bumpus as she traveled throughout France's countryside, is about people savoring the life they have been given.

Many Hands Make Light Work: A Memoir by Cheryl Stritzel McCarthy. $16.95, 978-1-63152-628-2. A rollicking family of nine children, offspring of an eccentric professor father and unflappable mother, paint, spackle, and eventually rebuild a dozen tumbledown old houses in their Midwest college town in the 1960s and '70s—and, at odd moments, break into song, because they sing as they work, like a von Trapp family in painters caps.

Milton Keynes UK
Ingram Content Group UK Ltd.
UKHW021334250923
429345UK00015B/66/J